MW01515666

BREAKING THE 9 TO 5 JAIL

Devesh Dwivedi

This book is for my father and mother; who taught me great work ethic. Thank you for inspiring me to work with purpose. I love you.

It takes a team to succeed, so thank you, team:

Anisha Sharma, Robert Louis Henry, Henry Tremain, Benier Koranache, and many more.

TABLE OF CONTENTS

Foreword 1

About This Book 2

Chapter 1: Entrepreneur in a 9 to 5 Jail 5
How Kelly Azevedo, An Accountant, Worked Herself Out of a Job
and Broke Free From the 9 to 5 Jail 23

Chapter 2: Playing Safe or Not Playing At All 26
How John Harthorne, a Strategy Consultant, Broke Free From the 9
to 5 Jail 49

Chapter 3: What It Takes 52
How Bhavin Parikh Went From Consultant to Entrepreneur 63

Chapter 4: Before You Break Away 66
How Aaron Schwartz Built Something of His Own To Break Out of
the 9 to 5 Jail 81

Chapter 5: Breaking the 9 to 5 Jail 83
How Nancy Nguyen Left the Structure of Suits and Time Clocks. 106

Chapter 6: The Hustle and the Leap 109
Jesse Pujji, An Investment Professional, Went After His Passions
Instead of Staying in the 9 to 5 Jail 119

Chapter 7: The Journey 123

How Aron Schoenfeld Went From Public Accountant to
Entrepreneur 138

Your 9 to 5 Escape Story 141

BONUS SECTION: More Success Stories 147

How Susan Strayer Stayed Connected With Her Employer Until She
Was Ready to Break Free From the 9 to 5 Jail 148

How Justin Beegel Left the Cubicle Life to Start an Infographics
Business 151

Her Corporate Job Wasn't So Bad, But Caroline Ghosn Saw
Potential in an Online Professional Network for Women 157

How Jim Garland Went From the Trunk of a Car to $3,500,000 .. 159

How Bonnie Buol Ruszcyzyk Went From Employee to Entreprenr
Despite Her Hardships 162

More From the Author 165

"If you live for weekends or vacations, your shit is broken."

– Gary Vaynerchuk

FOREWORD

Entrepreneurial success is not exclusively determined by your background, your education, or how much cash you have on hand. It is dictated by your beliefs. If you truly, emphatically believe you will succeed, you will. If you do not, you won't.

Right now, in this tough economy – when the unemployment rate is at an all-time high, when job security is a thing of the past, when companies are laying people off left and right – you have to take your future in your own hands.

Breaking The 9 to 5 Jail is a well-written, no-nonsense guide that lays out what you need to make a smooth transition from employee to entrepreneur. It gives you the inspiration, tools, resources, and guidelines to help you get started. Devesh Dwivedi is one of the new breed of entrepreneurs who recognizes that your time is now, and I can tell from his entrepreneurial stories, that he's a true "toilet paper entrepreneur" at heart. I am confident that this book will help you create a strong and successful business if you are willing to take the first step. If you truly want to flee the 9 to 5 jail, this book is the ideal escape map and Devesh would be your perfect accomplice.

Here's to getting rich right!

Mike Michalowicz,
The Toilet Paper Entrepreneur

Author of *The Toilet Paper Entrepreneur*, Mike has learned the hard way to weather the economic storm and come out on top. An international speaker and founder of three multi-million dollar companies before the age of 30, he knows how to start with nothing – with less than nothing – and do what's necessary to build a thriving business. He is a recurring guest on CNBC, National Public Radio (NPR), *New York Times*, and *Smart CEO Magazine*.

ABOUT THIS BOOK

"Do one thing every day that scares you."

— Eleanor Roosevelt

Get out - the time is RIGHT, the time is right NOW

The guiding principal behind this book is to give you an opportunity to reflect on your personal life, your 9 to 5 life, and help you make an educated decision about your career. This book is an opportunity for you to rethink why you are where you are and how to make the difference in your life that you have always dreamt about: starting a business of your own, being your own boss, and turning that idea that you have had in your head into a profitable business.

The fact that you are reading this book tells me you are either: a. unhappy and dissatisfied with your current job and want to be out as soon as you can or b. you want to start a business and want to make a smooth employee to entrepreneur transition. This book will help you in either case, as we will discuss the common reasons of job dissatisfaction and what you can do about it. Additionally, we'll cover strategies to smooth your employee to entrepreneur transition, if you choose to go that route. This book will show you how to establish a business and how to make time to work for yourself. This book will free you from working for others, who are stuffing their pockets, when you could work and earn for yourself and your family on your own terms.

Best of all, I'm going to help you break out of the 9-5 jail at your speed, time, and comfort level. All you have to do is simply read each chapter and follow the course of action suggested in the form of exercises and quizzes. Most importantly, for ongoing help and support, join our online community of aspiring entrepreneurs like you at www.breakingthe9to5jail.com

WARNING: Before we go any farther, let me warn you that:

ı Reading this book or any book or blog in the world will not help if you do not act. Action beats education. If you simply read book after book and blog after blog, and continue to just consume all the information without taking any action, then it is all a big waste of time. Business is more about doing and less about consuming information.

- Starting a business is a lot of hard work. It takes time, commitment, money, blood, tears, and sweat to start and build a business. Do not let the media's affection and sexiness around entrepreneurship seduce you into something that is not right for you.

This book is **NOT** for you if:

- You are looking for a get rich quick scheme or a six week program to financial freedom.

- You love your 9 to 5 job and your 9 to 5 boss!

- You want to continue working hard for others and building 'their' wealth.

- YOU think you are lucky to have a job.

- You do not like the idea of being your own boss.

Remember, while there are no shortcuts to SUCCESS, the journey is definitely worthwhile.

So, let's start... Shall we?

CHAPTER 1:
ENTREPRENEUR IN A 9 TO 5 JAIL

"The price of anything is the amount of life you exchange for it."
— Henry David Thoreau

Monday morning, 6AM, alarm clock goes off…

You hit the snooze button

Fifteen minutes later, the alarm goes off again…

What is the first thought in your head? What do you feel right at that moment, every morning? Are you excited to get up, start the day, and get to work? Or are you feeling like you have to drag yourself out of bed and to work?

You hit the snooze button a few too many times until you realize you are late for work, and you jump out of the bed screaming, "F…I'm late again… I hate my job!" You hurriedly get ready, rush to work, and try to sneak your way to your cubicle without getting caught by your boss and colleagues.

Is this your morning routine?

I know you have your own reasons for staying at this job and keep doing what you are doing, but I have only one question for you:

Is it worth getting up like this every morning, for the rest of your life?

Out of the 24 hours in a day, if we are lucky enough to get at least 8 hours of sleep and only 8 hours of work, then we are spending half of our waking hours working. Work is the only non-personal activity that we spend most of our time on. Work is where we spend most of our lives, and that makes it very important for us to enjoy the work, love what we do, have fun doing it, and not regret it every moment or complain about it to every other person.

I have yet to meet a kid who would answer, "I want to become an employee who sits in a cubicle and stares at a computer screen all day long when I grow up." The answers are usually: I want to be… an artist, a rock star, an astronaut, a scientist, an actor, a pilot, and so on. You probably answered something like that when you were a kid. Then what happened? Why and how did you end up in a cubicle with a mediocre life, average wages, and a horrible boss? Think about it!

In the most basic sense, we work to satisfy our basic needs (bread, butter, and shelter) and desires (vacations, comfort, and luxury). Some of us seek that in monthly paychecks and others in business ownership. To say one is better over the other would not be right unless the argument is in favor of the latter. A monthly paycheck may bring peace of mind to many of us. However, what is the point of such peace of mind if it comes with an insecurity that the paycheck can disappear any minute, leaving us miserable and with no control on our finances and career? That leads me to believe there are two groups – one that is risk averse; the one that does not want stress and pressure to perform that comes with freedom. They want to stay in a 9 to 5 jail peacefully ever after. They would compromise their long-term future and prosperity over short-term benefits (read paycheck next week). Then, there is another group of people; for them, the sky's the limit. They want to have it all! Jobs and a paycheck do not satisfy them. They would sacrifice the short-term benefits (paycheck) for long-term gains (ownership of finances, career, and life). They take risks to augment their lifestyles; they can not stop because life is not about flowing with the current, it's like sailing in the high seas.

So which group do you belong to? Do you just want to live peacefully (read scared of layoffs) paycheck after paycheck, or do you want to work and earn on your own terms? You have to decide.

Do You Hate Your Job?

This is, perhaps, the most important question in your life right now. Many people stuck in a 9 to 5 job hate it. They want freedom to do anything they want, whenever they want. There could be many reasons to hate a job: the boss, the pressure of deliverables, freeloader colleagues, the thought of being subservient to others, the lack of control, or the lack of reward, etc. Take a look at some of the widespread symptoms that indicate you are losing interest in your job, and it's easy to see that it may be time to do something about it.

- You are depressed every Sunday evening because the weekend is almost over and you have to work on Monday morning.

- You no longer enjoy and feel challenged in your job. It is either boring or of little interest to you.

- Your only goal is to get the work done as soon as possible, as opposed to doing the best job possible.

- All you care about is your paycheck and not about professional growth, future projects, or where the company is headed.

- You get to work late and leave early for no real reason other than you want to minimize your time spent at work.

- You look forward to the social interactions at work more than the actual work.

- You suffer "Grass is greener on the other side" syndrome (i.e. you feel that jobs, bosses, compensation, environment, and basically everything is better elsewhere and that it is only your job that is bad. This is rarely true, especially if this is the second or third job in a row that is making you feel this way.

- You feel like everyone enjoys being at work, while you do not, and you begin to resent your colleagues who are doing well in their jobs.

- You are only in your job because the economy is bad, and so you justify to yourself that there is no point in looking for another job.

- You spend too much time on non-work related stuff like surfing the web, celebrity gossip, blogging, stock trading, online shopping, and social networking sites like Twitter and Facebook.

If you suffer any of these symptoms or similar ones that give you a feeling of "I would rather be… (fill in your own thoughts)" while you are at work, then you are in a rut and on your way to becoming a disgruntled employee. You would be better off changing the job or career or starting your own business and creating an interesting job for yourself rather than doing nothing and harming yourself and your employer in the process. Do not wait for things to get better, because in most cases they won't.

Just because you hate your job does not qualify you for entrepreneurship.

Why Do You Hate Your Job?

Okay, so you hate your job. Well, first you need to find out why. You need to assess the reasons why you hate your job and determine if it's time to make a career change or an attitude change or jump ships or start a business of your own.

Take a structured approach to get a grip on the situation. Take some time to make a list of what you dislike about your job. You really must be specific. It is not just that you do not like your boss, but identify something you wish were different, e.g. the way he never gives you feedback or flies off the handle without reason, or never shares business information with you and your colleagues. Next, list what you like about your job. There must be something that you like, perhaps not your boss, but your colleagues, company, business, or your free health insurance. Compare the two lists; if there are more positive points, maybe it's time to resolve the negative. If not, then it's time for a change.

Give a closer look to the negatives now. Are you bored by what you do? Are you looking for more challenges or variety in work? Are you looking for a change in your career path? If the negatives are related to such issues, then depending on what the issues are, there are ways to work them out. Talk to your boss and tell him you could handle more and get involved in new projects. Take some evening classes to prepare for the career change. Volunteer to help colleagues and other teams. If that does not work, update your résumé and start looking for the job that fits your requirements and career path.

However, if the negatives are more in line with not being satisfied with personal achievements, not building a future, not having the freedom… then obviously, it's time to consider entrepreneurship as a career. In any case, if negative points outnumber positive ones, it's time to change. You might never get 100% satisfaction in any job in the world, and the best alternative is to create the job that you want!

Pay attention to the functional items on your list that bother you about your job, because these could stand in your way of success as an entrepreneur. Evaluate the personal problem areas. These are the problem items you need to address now because they will continue to be problems even when you are working for yourself. For example, if it's the long hours and weekend work that you are trying to get away from, then think again because you may very well be working late evenings and weekends for your own business too.

Point is, just because you hate your job does not qualify you for entrepreneurship. You should try to identify the reasons of your dissatisfaction and see if it is the job or you that is causing your issues. You should consider talking to a career counselor to find out if it's the career choices you have made that do not fit with your personality and if you are unhappy because of that. Maybe it is just time to jump ship or change careers and not really time to start a business.

Your Boss – Jail Warden

Bosses are the wardens of the 9 to 5 jail. They are always commanding what you do, how you do it, and how much you do every day. If needed, they will require you to work for 10-12 hours instead of eight. They will often require that you compromise your principles and upset your work-life balance. It's just business. They'll do anything to earn more money even if they have to 'detain' all their employees to work 80 hours a week.

For many of us, the idea of being supervised, ordered around, and pressured into work is really hard to accept. If you are a free spirit, you won't be able to work in one company for long. Not all bosses are bad. There are people who manage their sub-ordinates instead of commanding them. However, the idea of being your own boss and having things your way is irresistible. That's why Corporate is quickly transforming into Business and Self Employment. Many people leave their jobs each year to start a business just because they want to be their own boss!

Your Feelings

How does it feel when you go to work every day? Where do you see yourself next year and five years from now? What do you want from life? You should ask yourselves these questions and many more every day:

- Where do I stand in my career and life?
- Am I on the right path?
- Am I earning to my potential?
- Am I learning?
- Am I having fun doing what I do?
- Is my team supportive?
- Am I satisfied with my work?
- Am I growing?
- Am I happy with my work-life balance?
- Am I being challenged enough?

When it comes to your career, the most important thing is your feelings. Do you feel the seclusion and loneliness of a jail at your workplace? Do you feel 'detained' where your most amazing skills are cornered?

When you are ordered to do something, and you believe that is not the right thing to do or in best interest of the company or you or both, you feel lost and angry. This feeling takes a good portion of your rationality, and you start thinking about quitting. However, do not let your emotions overcome you, especially when you are angry, because anger usually leads to decisions that one most likely would regret later.

You also feel shackled when you want to exercise your skills and knowledge to solve a problem and your boss rejects you and your ideas. You are tired of hearing responses like "it does not work that way around here" or "that's not your job, so do not worry about it." The feelings become stronger when someone is stopping you from doing something you believe is right. The feelings grow stronger and stronger every day. But you should not let your momentary anger determine your future. Your decision should be carefully planned with all the pros and cons in mind.

Perhaps the most important question is how strong are your feelings about your present job situation? How content are you with the position you are in or the people you work for? The questions that you should be asking yourself right now are:

- Am I happy with my career path?
- Am I earning to my potential?
- Am I free?
- Am I learning and growing?

Am I Happy With My Career Path?

When you ask yourself this question, you will feel an uncertainty start swallowing up your senses. The career path that you took might not be akin to what you are good at. For example, you are passionate about cooking, but you are working as a receptionist for a big corporation. How happy could you be?

A lot of times, people choose odd careers that do not match their skills or what they wanted to do in their lives. They chose an odd career because it looked right at the time, and they didn't want to be left behind or miss the opportunity to earn money.

In essence, most of the people in a corporate 9 to 5 job are unhappy with their present situation. This effectively urges them to start their own business and do what they always wanted to do.

However, you need to answer this question with all the honesty. If you are happy with your career path and the job you are currently doing, you should keep it and get great joy and satisfaction from a job well done!

Once you realize what you want to do, and if that happens to be starting on your own; it is very easy to start your homework. In our example, the receptionist in a Fortune 100 company might begin pursuing a culinary degree in the evenings, start her own cooking show on the web, and/or begin working on a business plan for her own restaurant.

Am I Earning to My Potential?

Wouldn't you agree that a 9 to 5 job never made anyone rich? How many 9 to 5 employees make it or even stand a remote chance to make it to the lists like "Forbes' World's Richest People?" Think about it. (Let me give you a hint: NONE.)

For many people I have spoken with, money is evil. Let me rephrase: wanting more money is evil and something that is frowned upon. Well, that is the culture they purposefully build in corporations so they can save more on salaries and bump up their profits. Your income is their expense, and they want to keep that at the minimum they can get away with.

Now, it's true that not very entrepreneur gets in "world's richest" lists. The point is that it is very important for you to be happy with your compensation and potential for future growth in compensation. You should be making what you are worth, and there is nothing wrong with wishing and working for more. So the answer to this question will impact your career decision. And if pursuit of financial freedom is what you are looking for, it will strengthen your case if you decide to start a business.

Everyone wants a life of freedom and luxury. For some that might mean nice houses, fancy cars, expensive clothes, gourmet food, exotic wines, and travel! For others, it's the freedom and flexibility to take care of elderly parents, send their kids to the best universities, or retire to a picturesque beach house. Everyone wants the best in life, however they define it.

So if you want to stand a chance of achieving these dreams, working a 9 to 5 job might not be a good idea. How will you ever save enough to do all that? If money is the tool to acquire what you want in life, then you would have a better chance realizing those dreams as an entrepreneur instead of staring at a screen in your cubicle all day!

Am I Free?

Your spirit and your body are in chains because you are a corporate slave. You do not have the freedom to do anything you want. You do what your company wants you to do. Remember that job description you got? That's all you can do, and how you should do it is something your boss tells you. Freedom means that you can do what you want, whenever and however you want. For example, you are tired and want to take a vacation. You book the tickets and travel to the most exotic destination in the world. You can do this if you have your own business and have people handling various aspects of work for you.

If you are doing a 9 to 5 job, you have to ask for permission from your boss, and if your boss is not in a good mood, you won't be able to get permission. Now, you understand what slavery means in today's corporate world. If you like freedom to do what you want to do and rest when you want to rest, you should start planning your freedom. Breaking the 9 to 5 jail is not easy, but with careful planning and understanding, you can dash out of the 9 to 5 jail!

Am I Learning and Growing?

Are you in an environment where you are challenged enough everyday? Are you learning and growing from and with your work? Are you having fun doing what you are doing? Everyone has a gift, a special skill or talent, something we are naturally good at. Are you able to use that gift at your job?

If the answer to these questions, or even most of these questions, is *NO*, then why are you doing what you are doing? Why are you settling for less than you deserve? Let's take a look at self-employment or business ownership as a career option.

Your Business, Your Priorities

Consider what you value most. Is it your family, freedom to divide your time as you desire, or a large home by the lake front? What motivates you and drives you to be a successful professional? Before you quit your full-time job to start your own business, ask yourself how this change will impact your priorities. This is especially important for other people in your life who will be affected by your decision. Starting your own business is a time and energy consuming journey. To get your business off the ground and be successful, you will have to work hard and devote yourself to the business, sometimes at the sacrifice of other things of value.

For example, when I started my own business, there were priorities in my life that had to change. I had always made time for many social outings with lots of friends. During the start-up phase of my business, I attended many networking events and spent a lot of time making more business contacts, which left me less energized for socializing with friends. I experienced the proverbial "Entrepreneur's Loneliness" first hand and had to prioritize a few special friendships and only see other acquaintances at occasional events.

On the other hand, the benefits of being your own boss and doing everything on your own terms outweigh the efforts and sacrifices needed to start your own business. While your life may be hectic for a while, take comfort in knowing your work will be directly proportional to your reward. Does your 9 to 5 job allow for professional growth, financial security, and for salary increase proportionate to your performance at work? Does your job build an asset for you?

If you answered no, you should seriously consider starting your own business and regaining control over your life. You can now dedicate your time and energy to your own priorities instead of someone else's.

Your Business, Your Career

Knowing what you want to achieve in your career is critical to being successful, whether you own your own business or work for someone else. Having a goal in mind keeps you motivated to gain expertise in your industry and find new ways to improve your business.

Also, considering your long-term career goals can be a road map to discover whether you should leave your full-time job for a more independent lifestyle. Do you want to climb the corporate ladder with other professionals? Or are you more competitive as an individual, and more comfortable setting your own goals?

For example, as a Business Coach, I want to provide quality services, but I also want to be an inspiration to others and motivate them to succeed. I love working in different environments, with a diverse group of people, with new ideas. As an entrepreneur, I have more flexibility to achieve these goals than if I were working for a large corporation within the set boundaries of my cubicle and a job description. You have to consider where you want to be in five, ten, fifteen, twenty years, so you can get there successfully. If your long-term career objective includes running your own business, take the right steps to start. There are so many things you can do while you are working full-time: you can take the time to do some market research, take a marketing or accounting course at the local community college, test your idea as an evening and weekend business, start networking at events and associations in your niche, write your business plan, and secure financing for your small business.

The Magic of Working as Much as You Want

Perhaps the biggest reason to leave a job is to work as much as you want since you own the business and you set your own work hours. It is true that you have the freedom to earn as much money for yourself as you want and work accordingly. It is a fact that you have to work much harder – day and night – to establish a business. Normally, for the first couple of years, you might not find time for yourself – let alone having time to spend with family and friends.

If you are reeling from the fear of working hard in a business, consider the fact that a mother has to work harder to feed her baby when the baby is only a month old. She has to take care of the baby for the initial few years until he or she starts to understand and learn how to take care of him/herself. A startup business is like a newborn: the most painful part is birth, i.e. starting, taking the first step and of course you have to work harder to nourish it and raise it initially, and then as the time passes and you put together a system that functions, the business runs itself and you manage it just a like a proud parent manages their grownups. Of course there are differences in managing kids and business, because your teenage daughter may tell you that she is an adult and may even start making her own decisions, which your business will not do. So rest assured your business would be far more obedient than teenage kids!

Once the business is set up and running smoothly, you will be freed up to spend time with family or go on vacation. First, you need to dedicate time and energy to establish and scale your business. Once your business is scaled and systemized, you will definitely be able to decide your hours, time off, and choose to work as much as you want.

Working Hard to Receive a Bonus

In a 9 to 5 job, you work hard 8 hours a day, 5 days a week (if you are lucky, and many 9 to 5 employees are not that lucky, working longer hours and more days per week is the norm for them). The hard work and achievements entitle you to a bonus. The bonus is often peanuts compared to your hard work and achievement. Let me give you a simple example. I know one company where an employee would, at the end of the year, get a bonus based on the number of hours worked over and above the expected 40 hours. There is a long table of what the bonus amount would be depending upon how much more the employee worked over the 40 hours a week. I'll pick one to keep it simple: a $5,000 annual bonus for those who worked an average of 45hr/week. Let's assume that this employee has a salary of $60,000 annual. Now, let's do the math:

Salary: $60,000
Hours expected: 40X52 = 2,080hrs
Average salary per hour: = $60,000/2,080hrs = $28.85/hr
Bonus: $5,000
Hours expected: 5X52 = 260hrs
Average bonus per hour: $5000/260hrs = $19.23/hr

Wait a minute! So, you have been working harder and harder, staying late at work to earn this bonus, and it's not even equal to your average per hour wage, let alone being higher to motivate you. Is this really a bonus?

Try analyzing your company's bonus structure and requirements, and you will see 9 out of 10 times, the bonuses are not well defined or explained, and at the end, they are not the motivating carrot they should be.

In business, your profit is your bonus. You work hard every day to expand your business, lift your bottom line up, and ultimately make a profit. This in turn encourages you to work even harder to take your business to the next level.

In the process, you make more money and eventually lead a lifestyle you always wanted – a lifestyle of wealthy people! Riches bring freedom to do what you want, when you want, how you want, and freedom to make choices, call all the shots, and enjoy the race instead of running it for someone else. Do not get me wrong, entrepreneurship is not just about the money and wealth, but remember that money does play a very critical role in life.

The Ultimate Bonus

Bonuses are a part of 9 to 5 jobs. They are an effective way to motivate you to do your best for the company. A corporation can never be successful without its workforce. To keep the workforce happy, companies dole out bonuses.

Receiving bonuses once a year may help you save some money. But in most cases, you already have plans on how you are going to spend the money on Christmas gifts, or that big kitchen remodeling due for months now. This once per year cash may bring momentary happiness in your present job. You may feel briefly motivated to work even harder to receive more bonuses in future, but do not let these small rewards keep you away from the biggest reward ever – the reward of having the control over rewards, the reward of being your own boss.

The ultimate bonus is not when an employer gives you some extra money for your work. It is the sheer feeling that sweeps over you when your business wins that big project that you have been working and waiting months for. The satisfaction and accomplishment that only a business owner or a parent can feel when they see their business or child grow and do well.

If you think a 401k plan, juicy bonuses each year, and occasional employee awards are the best thing that could happen to you, you should think again. Being an entrepreneur comes with so much more than 401k plans, bonuses, and awards. You have complete control over your money, and you simply cannot put a price tag on the feeling of entrepreneurial accomplishment that dwarfs any reward in the corporate world.

Once you establish your business, the pure joy and freedom of being your own boss and running your own show will be 100 times better than receiving a bonus after working hard days and nights for a full year. And remember, you are the boss, so reward your employees, customers, associates, and yourself whenever and however you want.

Freedom!

Entrepreneurship is all about freedom. These 9 to 5 jobs are like barriers that do not let you fly higher. In your own business, you set yourself free. You do what feels right. You employ all your skills to earn more money for yourself. There is no limit to how much you can earn. The harder and smarter you work, the better your business will be.

However, if you think that business is risky and job is peace of mind, you are absolutely wrong. Business is risky, but a job even riskier. How many people do you know who have unexpectedly lost a job at some point in their career? Are you immune to this fate? At least as an entrepreneur, you have full visibility into the risks and you can work around the products, services, business model, strategy to get out of the unpleasant situations that employees cannot.

So, remember that "Opportunity favors the bold." And business is the opportunity that favors only the courageous people who will do anything to succeed. They eventually win. A business may be more stressful than a day job, but in the end, it has far more satisfaction than any corporate job.

The next chapter, **Playing it 'Safe' or Not Playing At All**, addresses the very common pitfall where aspiring entrepreneurs fall into the whole trap of procrastination and the best excuse they came up with is, "I'm playing it safe…" Let's talk about playing safe, but first, take this 10 question exercise to find out if you are ready to break the 9 to 5 Jail…

⚲ Now Take Action! #1: Entrepreneur in the 9 to 5 Jail? ⚲

Answer the following on a scale of 1 to 5, 1 being Strongly Disagree and a 5 being Strongly Agree.

Question	Score
I enjoy not knowing day to day what my work tasks might be.	
I can handle surprises well and prefer the adventure of an unpredictable day.	
I do not need clear direction to perform a task successfully.	
I really dislike my boss and have a poor relationship with him/her.	
I feel my suggestions and ideas at work are never valued or implemented.	
I do not feel motivated by the compensation, benefits, and bonus offerings at my job.	
I like making all the decisions to complete a business task and being personally responsible for the outcomes.	
I prefer a work environment that is fluid and challenging.	
I get more satisfaction from receiving positive feedback in the form of bonuses than in the form of praise from my boss and peers.	
Based on what I read in this section, my life is well positioned to break out of the 9 to 5 jail.	
Total	

Once you are done, look at the score interpretations below.

Score	Interpretation
10 - 25	Starting a business is not the best idea for you right now. Perhaps in the future, you will be better suited to take this step, but for now, enjoy your job and find ways to continue learning and growing so you will be ready when the time is right to strike out on your own.
25 - 40	You are on the fence, and you should take more time to review your skills, your situation, and the timing for taking such a big risk. Keep reading so you know ways that you can prepare yourself. You may feel quite different in a year or two.
40+	You are in the 9 to 5 jail, and it's time to break free!

HOW KELLY AZEVEDO, AN ACCOUNTANT, WORKED HERSELF OUT OF A JOB AND BROKE FREE FROM THE 9 TO 5 JAIL

Kelly Azevedo was so efficient at her corporate job, she worked herself out of a full-time job. See how she escaped the 9 to 5 jail and created her own, efficient-running business.

Who are you and what kind of corporate job were you at?

My name is Kelly Azevedo, and I was working in accounting for a company managing 35 care facilities in northern California. In addition to managing the finances of the homes, I created the systems and structures around the office and our accounting process. The more that I refined and developed the system, the more I realized that I really enjoyed designing the system but became bored doing the same thing day after day. I suggested to my manager that I incorporate into more areas of the business to improve our marketing and insurance practices.

What made you leave the job? When did you realize that you wanted to be an entrepreneur and why?

My manager sat me down for my performance review only to say that I exceeded all expectations and because I was so efficient they were cutting my hours back by 20% (and thus my pay). I was already looking into working with entrepreneurs, and that was the push I needed to commit to get out of a bad situation.

What did you do to break the corporate jail? How did you prepare for the employee to entrepreneur transition?

After doing some free work, I transitioned to working for a paying client until the hours requested built up and I could transition to contracting fulltime. I was enjoying the contract work much more than my desk job, both in working with entrepreneurs who were creating new programs and in the flexibility that such work afforded. If I had the chance to do it all again, I'd spend more time transitioning and ensuring I had more depth in my client base before making the leap.

What is one resource (person, coach, book, organization anything) that helped the most/best?

The top resource was actually a client who coached entrepreneurs and who I was able to shadow and learn from as I developed my own business while supporting as a contractor. Many coaches provide free content and informational calls, which were invaluable when it came to learning about the coaching available and who I wanted to work with to grow my business.

What do you know now that you wish if only you knew when you made the transition?

I wish I'd known more about how to get clients through marketing (advertising, word of mouth, speaking, SEO, all the avenues) and that it takes an investment of energy and effort over time to get consistent results. Marketing is a process that will be on-going throughout your business, so the sooner you begin testing what is most effective for your audience, the quicker you get results.

Any suggestions for aspiring entrepreneurs?

Read and learn from a variety of entrepreneurs - most have content and training available so you can experience their work without investing money upfront. When you've implemented the free material and you're ready to invest in this business be sure to complete your due diligence before signing up for a program. In the beginning it's easy to get star struck and invest in the wrong program or coach for your business. There are many people who serve entrepreneurs, and it takes time to find the right person who teaches someone at your level. There's a huge leap between beginning marketing practices and detailed campaigns for an established company or brand - invest in the wrong one and you're wasting time and money!

How are you doing and how do you feel now?

It's a completely different viewpoint and mindset being an entrepreneur. You're responsible for so much more than showing up and being present for 8 hours but the rewards are phenomenal! I'm working with clients who are taking their six-figure businesses to seven-figure or their million dollar businesses to multi-millions. It's fast paced, fun, challenging work and I enjoy it immensely. It's wonderful to feel in control of your business, career and ultimately life, and there's equal parts pride and joy in creating the life I want for myself. As you grow from employee to entrepreneur the support systems and mentors will show up if you're looking for and accepting of their support.

Key Takeaway

Kelly Azevedo had the gumption to leave her 9 to 5 jail after getting a reduction in hours and pay. She took her life and work into her own hands. Instead of allowing herself to be punished for doing a great job and doing it efficiently, she said, "I'm done," while walking out the door. Sometimes you need that push to get you off your feet and into action mode.

CHAPTER 2:
PLAYING SAFE OR NOT PLAYING AT ALL

"If God only gave me a clear sign, like making a large deposit in my name at a Swiss bank."
– Woody Allen

Playing Safe?... or Not Playing at All?

We all think about our future, career, and money for most of our life. We see ourselves rich and live a perfect life in our dreams. Most of us only dream about an independent life full of happiness and riches; very few of us actually stand up and start working to achieve our dreams and make it real. Those who work hard to achieve their dreams are people who understand that working to make dreams a reality is the only way to achieve those dreams. If you keep on thinking about starting a business, talking about making plans, but do not act on it, you are among those who can only dream.

Come Play

Are you playing it safe or just NOT playing in the name of playing it safe? Are you scared of playing? What is it that you are fearful of, or what is it that's stopping you from playing?

Ask this question to yourself and answer honestly, too.

Let's accept it; you will never be able to play unless you get out on the field, a practice cage, or a driving range.

You see, traditional wisdom advised (and still does) to go to college, get good grades, get a job with a big company, and retire with as much money as possible. But there's a new (and there's always been) breed of worker − the budding entrepreneur. They are the ultimate risk-takers − they leave large, to live large. And, there are some who do want to leave but cannot because of whatever reason − mostly fear of failure, or of success, perhaps. Fear is understandable, but as an individual and an aspiring entrepreneur, you need to do some self assessment and figure out what your fears are. Are you playing safe, i.e. planning and making efforts toward a successful exit from the rat race. Or are you just rationalizing your fears and excuses and have accepted (maybe in your subconscious) that you are staying in the rat race forever? If you really want to make a successful exit from modern day slavery, you need to openly talk about those excuses with which you rationalize your fears. You need to talk about the education and information that you need to overcome those fears and deal with the excuses you have been giving to yourself. You need to find more people like you, bring them all together, and work together to help each other.

Let's accept it; you will never be able to play unless you get out on the field, a practice cage, or a driving range. So, you have to set your fears aside and get into the game. It works the same way in business. How can you do business when you are afraid of business? Business means risk, calculated risk. If you are afraid of taking a calculated risk, you should reconsider entrepreneurship.

If you convince yourself that the hundreds of books, blogs, and podcasts you have consumed over the past so many years are in preparation for that glorious day when you will tell your boss to stick it in his ear, you are wasting your time. Do not read another book or blog post about startups or entrepreneurship unless you take action. Once you are done reading this book (or even before), go out and start building something (a product, a blog, a company) of your own. Experience is the best learning.

But if you realize that one of the pleasures in your life is to read about code, startups, entrepreneurs, music, then accept that you are a consumer. Knowledge for knowledge's sake is not bad, as long as you realize that you are not working toward an end beyond your own edification, which again, is not a bad thing.

Likewise, if you are someone who has an unquenchable desire to produce something, then stop reading about other people and start doing it yourself. Seriously, do not read another blog post, tweet, or issue of Entrepreneur magazine until you have made an evident move toward that goal to which you so desperately aspire. Once you have made that single action toward advancing your idea, you can come back and read and research, which will help you toward your goals. So let's recap:

If you have been reading startup books and blogs for years and never started anything, it's time to accept that your tendency is to be a consumer. It's not to say you cannot break out of that classification by starting something, but if you have not done it thus far, you are not likely to do it soon without some external motivation. Maybe this book will be the catalyst you have been waiting for!

If you have fifty ideas and your hard drive is littered with folders containing thirty lines of plan for each, you tend toward being a consumer (or at least a producer who has trouble finishing things). And if you figure out that you are a producer, stop daydreaming about the day you will make things happen. Start making it happen in the next 30 days, or forever hold your peace!

So stop thinking about the big day when you will make everything happen, stop reading books and blogs and other stuff, and start making it happen. Action is what counts.

Playing-it-Safe is NOT Playing at All

Taking risks is part of life. You have the ability to make things happen, and you are ready to start, but then you start thinking about playing it safe. Obviously, not everyone starting a business has buckets full of money. Everyone thinks about the risks involved. As humans, we rationalize our fears and uncertainties by calling it 'playing it safe.' You would never know what problems you can face, and how to solve them, if you never act. The key is to move on and start acting – in this case, start a business. Problems will come, but there will be ways to solve them, and eventually, those problems will fade away and new exciting challenges will replace them.

So, if you are afraid of losing time and your job, shrug it off, because it will only make you lose them for sure. Of course, you need to play it safe, but making it an excuse for not starting a business keeps you locked up in the 9 to 5 jail. Now, let's look at some of the very common excuses:

- I am ready to start a business, but I do not know how to keep my job and start a business at the same time.

- I want to start a business, but there are too many risk involved.

♀ I have created a business plan, but I do not know how to get the finances together.

 ♀ I am still researching the market.

 ♀ My significant other does not agree on starting a business.

 ♀ My friends think I am not a business type.

 ♀ I want to break the 9 to 5 jail, but I do not know how to start a business.

 ♀ I am confused about the type of business I can handle. I am good at making coffee!

 ♀ I do not have enough finances to start a business.

 ♀ There is a lot of competition in my niche. I could never succeed.

 ♀ I do not know how to research my target market

If you have any of the above excuses, then I am here to rescue you. In the coming pages, I'll be addressing each one of these excuses, which will help you re-think your situation. I am answering each excuse with a solution; however, I would encourage you to make a list of your own excuses and work around them. So, here it goes:

I am ready to start a business, but I do not know how to keep my job and start a business at the same time.

It's a good idea to keep your job while starting a business. However, if you have enough savings to sustain yourself for a year, you can ditch your job. There is no need to take on extra burden.

Start by doing extensive market research. For example, you want to open a restaurant that serves small portions of food. Visit the local market to learn more about the availability and costs of your inventory. Check the restaurants that are offering small food portions and think of ways you can improve upon the idea. Do this after your job hours. For example, instead of going home and watching TV after work, you can be working on your new business! Do some informal market research by discussing the idea with your friends and family. Do formal market research by looking online for any resource available that shows data for your target market, annual spending, success rate in your category, etc. You can also spend weekends putting together your plan and identifying areas where you will need funding and help; perhaps you can even run an ad for a chef partner and begin interviewing, as well as visiting local properties you might consider as the restaurant's location.

When you feel you are ready to take the next steps, you can always take a few days of vacation to take care of matters that need your physical presence. If you have enough investment, you can hire others to handle such details for you. Alternatively, you can ask your spouse, cousin, or friend to help you in your side gig.

I want to start a business, but there are too many risks involved.

Every business involves risks. There is not a single business in the real world that does not involve risks. You need to calculate the risk involved and know how much tolerance you have for risk before getting started.

Jot down the risks you or your loved ones perceive in starting a business. Write a potential solution for each risk. For example, if you mention that leasing a place for your business is expensive and risky, write down the solution, such as, "Work out of my spare room until the first contract is signed" or "check places that have lower rent" or "find a small business who would sublet some space" whatever fits your need and budget.

You will be amazed how easy it is to find a solution once you identify the risks. Address each risk on a separate piece of paper – this way you can address them one at a time and not feel overwhelmed by the sum of all risks together. If you think you can lose money in starting a business, you need to re-think about starting a business altogether.

By managing your finances, you can reduce the risk of losing money. I will address this one in the upcoming section.

I have created a business plan, but I do not know how to get the finances together.

The finances are the biggest problem in starting a business, but with patience and diligence, they can easily be sorted out. Your business is your baby, so you have to pay for it, at least until you have an investor. And the first thing an investor looks for is what have you, the business owner, invested? If you are not ready to risk your own money, why would an investor do so? So be prepared to invest at the initial stage. Consider bootstrapping, partnerships, loans, and non-traditional ways to fund your business

Money has two sides, either earn more or spend less (read smart). Always remember, a penny saved is a penny earned. So, in addition to securing more and more finance, what would help you is to spend your money wisely.

First, you need to know how much you need to invest in your startup. Open a separate account for the business and put all the money you intend to invest in your business, in that account. Be smart while spending money. Look for cost effective alternatives and always go for economic alternatives that offer acceptable quality. It is ok to have used furniture or equipment as long as they are usable. Look for other startup businesses and service providers to find the best bargains. Always ask for receipts when you purchase anything for your business. Add up the receipts and keep track of all your spending. Not only would this help you with taxes (remember the tax deductions for business expenses) at the year end, but looking back at your expenses, you would know specifically where you wasted money and where it was well spent.

Too many entrepreneurs fail before they even have a customer, because they've gone out and bought a new mahogany desk, fancy gold name plates, and top of the line printers, fax machine, stationary, and business cards. Depending on your business, you can probably accomplish the same work from your dining room table, an occasional trip to Kinkos, and do-it-yourself perforated business cards on a home inkjet computer – all at a fraction of the cost. When you close that first big deal (or perhaps the second or third,) then you can reward yourself with the office of your dreams.

If you think you are not good at finances, ask someone you trust, such as a friend or a relative, to help you out with finances. Remember, you can do more with less, if you manage your finances effectively.

I am still researching the market.

It's true that researching a market takes time, but if you have been "researching" for an extended period of time now, it's time for an excuse check. You need to systemize the research process, document it, and write action steps. You, alone, cannot research the market effectively. Ask your friends and family to help you out with the research. Tap into local resources that are free, such as the library or a local small business development center (SBDC) in US and the Business Link (TBL) in Canada. It's easy to break into a niche that is already popular than a niche that is unique. You can always innovate in a popular niche, but to create a niche of your own needs lot of work (educating the customers), patience, money, and time!

Research time depends on your business idea and how much time you are spending every day, but I recommend not spending more than a month to research. Get started as soon as you have done some basic research and validated that your idea is legal, market opportunity exists, and how you'll make money with it. It might take a bit more for some businesses, but typically a month is sufficient. You should continue to do market research after you have started your business so you can always be on top of the latest trends in consumer needs and expectations. This is the only way to stay ahead of your competition.

To systemize the research process, you have to break it into three categories and address each separately: Market Research, Supply and Demand, and Market Forecast.

The market research process means you visit your competitors and check the popularity of the product/service you intend to offer. Check the number of competitors in your area. This is important since you need to offer unique product/service that will pique the market's interest.

Study the supply and demand. Is there enough demand for your product (if any)? Is the current supply enough to meet the market demand? These and other questions need to be addressed. Investors and lenders will look for solid answers to these questions before they are willing to hand over their money.

Then, you need to research the future of the market. Check the stock market, talk to customers and see what they would want to see in future, and watch trends and market shifts in closely related industries. This study would give you a sense of direction for your business' future.

My spouse does not agree on starting a business.

If your better half is reluctant, you need to convince her/him. The best way is to communicate and help your spouse understand why you feel you are in a 9 to 5 jail and ask for their help to escape.

It is always good to discuss your business plan with your spouse. Your spouse is your number one stakeholder, and I cannot emphasize enough how important it is for your business, as well as personal life, to have their support. Listen to your spouse' concerns, if he or she is reluctant to cooperate, then there should be a reason for it.

Discuss your business plan/action plan with your spouse. Demonstrate that the business you are starting is going to be profitable and provide for other things that the two of you have dreamt about together, like a great home, reliable retirement, flexibility to spend more time with the family and friends, etc.

Discuss with family members and get their opinions; write them down and thoughtfully consider and address their resistance. They may identify a challenge you have not thought of. Make the final decision based on these discussions, and let your family members know about it.

The ideal way is to give a small presentation to your family. This way, you will be able to assert your point vocally. The whole idea is to convince them that starting a business is far more profitable than working 9 to 5 in a corporate jail. The presentation should be based on your business plan. This is a good way to practice your presentation skills since you will need these when you present your case in front of customers, investors, and other stakeholders. It will stir confidence in you, so you are killing two birds with one stone.

My friends think I am not a business type.

You have to find out what your friends think? This is one of the most obvious signs of indecisive nature. This is your life, and this is your future. If you can not decide for yourself, you should reconsider your ability to sit in the driver's seat of a business.

Self-confidence and decisiveness are the most important traits you need to have if you want to start your own business. It is not advisable to start a business if you aren't assertive and your ability to make a decision is non-existent.

If you want to convince your friends that you have what it takes to be a successful business owner, and they are important to you, give them a presentation. Show them what you have done and how excited you are to start a business of your own. Ask them to help you in research, to encourage you along the way, and to hold you accountable when the going gets tough.

You do not need to convince others to make a decision. There are people who will never agree with you no matter how sound your decision is or how cool your idea sounds. They will find a way to contradict and discourage you. Ignore those naysayers. In most cases, the biggest haters are the guys who never did anything themselves, and they want the rest of the world to be just like them. Whenever you see a naysayer, just look at him and ask yourself, do you want to end up being like him? Is he someone you see as a role model? If your answer is yes, follow his advice, and if the answer is no, ignore the guy and whatever advice he has to offer.

For example, early on in my business, I took pride in being nice to everyone by giving everyone a listen and trying to please everyone. The problem was that listening to all the naysayers meant I spent a lot of time doing nothing because I was afraid to act on what I wanted to do. The only thing I gained was loads of regret and lost opportunities. Remember, a journey of a thousand miles starts with one step. Action is what counts, so take action even if there are people who advise you to do it differently. It's your business; you have got to do what you think is best.

I want to break the 9 to 5 jail, but I do not know how to start a business.

Do not worry. This is exactly what this book helps you with. The key feeling is there: you want to break out of the 9 to 5 jail. All you need is the right direction toward your goals.

Starting a business is not as difficult as many think. All it takes is a proper action plan, persistence, patience, and execution to make a business successful.

Take the example of any successful entrepreneur today. They were (and are) just normal people like the rest of us. They made decision and never procrastinated. They took calculated risks and became extremely successful!

Remember, you have to take action! That is the key. No delays, no waiting for the right time. You need to start today. The time is right, and the time is RIGHT NOW.

However, if you are concerned that you cannot handle a business, start small, reassess your skills along the way, and do not give up. You never know what your hidden talent is.

I am confused about the type of business I can handle. I am good at making coffee!

Take a stock on your skills, education, background, hobbies, and what you are good at. Make a list of tasks you enjoy or subjects that get you fired up. Start digging deeper to identify a business idea that fits nicely with your skill sets and interests, as well as the demand in the market. As you evaluate the things on your list, cross out those you are not sure about. If you end up with two or three options, choose one you like the most. (Please read the **8 Escapes** section in **Chapter 5 – Breaking The 9 to 5 Jail**, to learn more about different options and how to get started.)

Be careful about deciding to start a business based on a hobby. Some have had success at this, but many discover that passion for a hobby does not necessarily translate into a successful business. There is a reason why we enjoy our hobbies, but if we had to make a living doing what we enjoy as a hobby, the hobby all of a sudden becomes your vocation, and you may not enjoy it as much.

Each one of us has a special talent; every one of us loves to do one thing or another, and we are naturally good at it. For example, you might like cooking. Start a small restaurant or party catering business. Do what you always loved to do, besides sleeping and watching TV!

I do not have enough finances to start a business.

If you do not have enough finances, you can always seek loans, partnership, and investment. There are a variety of funding options available for budding entrepreneurs. Depending on the size of your requirements, you can consider starting it out with your own credit cards or personal line of credit, or friends and family, loan from a bank, or invite someone to be a partner. If you have a technology and/or innovation based business with potential for scalability, then you may even consider pitching your idea to the local business Incubators, or Angels' network, or VC (Venture Capitalists) firms.

There are local groups, Government and not-for-profit organizations (Small Business Association, Canadian Youth Business Foundation, Canada Small Business Financing Program) that support new entrepreneurs and lend money on much simpler terms and offer lower interest rates as well. Banks also give business loans, but this can be a little challenging unless you have good personal credit history or collateral to offer.

Draft an estimate that gives you a clear idea of the resources that you will need to start your business. For example, let's say you need $40,000 to start a do-it-yourself printing shop. A good place to start would be to ask your friends and family for a loan on easy terms. If they do not have the money or they do not want to give you a loan, go for local banks and organizations that might be able to fund your idea. But first, do your homework! Go through these steps to compile your case:

- ໃ Write a solid business action plan that covers every aspect of the business – problems, solutions, demand, supply, competitors, etc. – as well as documents your course of action for the near future.

- ໃ Compile a feasibility report that validates the feasibility and profitability of your business

- ໃ Create a PowerPoint presentation based on the business plan.

- ໃ Present your case to potential funders and investors to convince them with what is in it for them.

There is a lot of competition in my niche. I could never succeed.

This is wrong! You can succeed in any niche in the world. Take a look at the restaurant business. How many restaurants are there in your area? There are probably 7 to 10 restaurants serving really good food. Does this discourage people to open more restaurants? Not at all!!

All you need is a good idea and excellent execution. Or an innovative approach that's better than what and how everyone else is offering the same products or services. If you want to jump in business, you should have an exceptional idea and lots of enthusiasm coupled with realistic market research matched with a dynamite market opportunity.

Success never comes overnight. You have to work at it. Check out the Wikipedia articles for the history and background of the fastest growing companies of recent times – Facebook, Google, Amazon, Yahoo, Apple, and Microsoft, etc. – and you will find the founders of those companies weathered several years of hard work, financial losses, and criticism before they saw any considerable success.

Competition validates the existence of an opportunity. If a niche has a lot of competition, you can be assured there is a lot of money to be made in that niche. Small or no competition simply means there is not enough opportunity or money to begin with.

So you need to research your market and create a sound marketing plan that drives people's attention to your product. Remember, you can get their attention if your product is unique and provokes curiosity among the masses. Use out of the box (better break that darn box) ways to draw attention. Not every strategy can strike gold for you. You need to test marketing strategies. Keep what's useful and discard the rest. Experimenting is the key.

I do not know how to research my target market.

Understanding your target market of potential customers is vital to starting a business that really sells. And making assumptions about what those potential customers want is a dangerous game to play, so it's important to do some digging and learn directly from them. Find out what their interests and needs are and how much they would be willing to spend for your particular product or services. You might be surprised by what you learn!

Some of the key things you need to learn about your target market include:

- Demographics: age, gender, occupation, income, geographic location

- Size: annual revenue of competitors, market projections for new products

- Future: five or ten years predictions for the market size

- Sub-Groups: sub-groups within the target market

⸙ Interests: what interests them the most and tickles their buying bone?

Your first stop for information about your target market should be your local library. Many of the sources from which you derive your competitive market analysis are also great sources of data on the people you hope will buy your product or service.

Beyond publicly available research, the primary means of gathering invaluable, specific information about your target audience is by conducting surveys and focus groups, and you can do both for a lot less than you think.

⸙ Now Take Action! #2: It's Time to Tackle Your Excuses! ⸙

Make a list of all the excuses you are making to not move forward in pursuing your entrepreneurial dreams.

Now, for each one, think about what aspects are legitimate and write those out. Are you sure? Are you making assumptions, or have you thoroughly considered the situation? For instance, your friends may indeed all think you are not a business type. But if none of your friends have experience running a business, they may not be the best source of confidence at this point. Go to a local business development center and speak with someone who is a seasoned business owner and get his perspective on what it takes to be successful. Then you can better decide for yourself whether you feel you have those traits.

For each excuse, write out an action statement asserting how you will overcome that excuse. You can use the list on next page or make a list of your own excuses

Excuse	Possible Solutions	Action Step
1. I am ready to start a business, but I do not know how to keep my job and start a business at the same time.		
2. I want to start a business, but there are too many risks involved.		
3. I have created a business plan, but I do not know how to get the finances together.		
4. I am still researching the market.		
5. My spouse does not agree on starting a business.		
6. My friends think I am not a business type.		
7. I want to break the 9 to 5 jail, but I do not know how to start a business.		
8. I am confused about the type of business I can handle. I am good at making coffee!		
9. I do not have enough finances to start a business.		
10. There is a lot of competition in my niche. I could never succeed.		
11. I do not know how to research my target market.		
12. Give me time and I'll come up with more excuses.		

I have no more excuses.

Are you out of excuses? Well, now that all your excuses and objections have been addressed, it's time to bust some of the popular myths around small business and startups.

Business Myths – Facts or Lies?

There are people who consider business as the only way to earn loads of money. While this is true, you need to understand that starting a business and building it is not as easy as everyone thinks. It requires a lot of work, patience, persistence, and determination. Consider some of the business myths and the reality behind them:

Myth #1: A brilliant idea will make me rich.

Reality: A brilliant idea is neither necessary nor sufficient for a successful business, although everything else being equal, it would give you some leverage. My personal opinion is that an idea alone is worth nothing, we all have so many every day. Look at it this way, your idea cannot even buy you a cup of coffee. If you do not agree with me, go to a potential investor and ask for a signed NDA (Non Disclosure Agreement), and you will know how much any idea is worth. Remember, there are millions of 'idea' people, and from them come billions of ideas. The only ones that count are those that come from the person who had the next big idea and he or she actually took the first step, risked time and money to build a valid prototype/proof of that idea, and literally created the hunger amongst VCs, angel investors, and/or incubators to take a bite on the idea.

Myth #2: I need a lot of money to start my business.

Reality: Well, I'm not sure what business you are starting that needs "a lot" of startup investment (plus we all have our own definition of "a lot"). Mike Michalowicz, author of the bestseller *the Toilet Paper Entrepreneur*, has written extensively about bootstrapping, so I won't belabor it too much, except to say this: you do not need much startup capital, but what you do need is a willingness to work. You have to bring your brilliant idea to fruition yourself; no one else will do it for you, and no one will give you the money to hire someone to do it for you. It's very simple logic: if I am not investing and hence risking my own time and money on my own idea, how could I expect someone else to? What level of self-confidence and sincerity does that show?

Myth #3: I do not need a business plan, because it's all in my head.

Reality: Having the business plan in mind but not on paper is the most common and worst of the myths with small business owners. Many of us fail to recognize the difference between ideas and plans.

You think you have the plan in your head, but my dear friend, let me break the News to all who think they have a plan in their head. No, you do not! All you have inside your head are ideas, ideas of and about your business. These ideas need to be brainstormed and documented for effective and profitable implementation.

I've seen many entrepreneurs talking for hours and hours about their business, but when asked to write a precise statement about who is their target market and how will they reach out to them, they will shy away. That does not mean they do not know what they are talking about. It's just one more sign of no plan of action and no direction. These folks with so many ideas but no concise plan tend to start a lot but accomplish little, so do not be one of them.

Myth #4: Someone will steal your idea if you do not protect it.

Reality: Honestly, unless you have discovered the cure to cancer or something ground breaking, your idea is not at risk. Millions of 'idea' people with billions of ideas think that their idea is the best. There's nothing wrong with protecting your idea, but we need to be a bit practical. So, get over the myth that people are after stealing your business idea.

I personally believe protecting an idea is challenging because there are so many legal ways that someone can do exactly what you are doing, which totally defeats the purpose of protection in the first place. Also, most investors claim they invest more in the person than the idea. Your energy, excitement, and enthusiasm to make that idea work, which none of the copycats have, is the real differentiator.

I do understand and realize the importance of protection and first to market advantage, so I highly recommend doing some research. Check out the U.S. Patent and Trademark Office at www.uspto.gov and the U.S. Copyright Office website at www.copyright.gov or Canadian Intellectual Property Office at www.cipo.ic.gc.ca to find the right information and explore your options for such protection.

Myth #5: I will be able to write everything off.

Reality: This is a mistaken belief. Yes, you can write off many business-related expenses that are directly related to your business. Tax time brings quite a surprise for many entrepreneurs who expected to be able to include many personal expenses as well. Doing some research into the types of expenses you can deduct will help you file the correct taxes and avoid a tax audit in the future. I would highly recommend spending some time on the tax department websites like IRS (Internal Revenue Service) website at www.IRS.gov, and CRA (Canadian Revenue Agency) at www.cra-arc.gc.ca as well as consulting a qualified accountant on tax matters.

Myth #6: I will be able to get a government grant to start my business.

Reality: Again, sorry to break the bad News, but there is no such program that gives FREE money to start businesses. Grants are generally tied to a social, scientific, and/or economic cause in some way or another. They are not made to enrich an individual or business. You should research and find other programs like tax breaks or subsidy for job creation, supporting a particular industry in your area that otherwise is almost extinct, scientific research and development tax credits etc.

Your best bet would be an SBA (Small Business Administration) or CSBF (Canada Small Business Financing Program) loan, if you can get one. Look at www.SBA.gov or www.ic.gc.ca/csbfp for information on loan options and the eligibility requirements.

Myth #7: I need an MBA to be a successful entrepreneur.

Reality: I had two successful businesses before I went to B-School for an MBA. An MBA shows you are willing to put up with the grueling effort it takes to struggle your way through a challenge, but is not a guarantee or a requirement for success.

By the way, the founders of Apple Computer, Microsoft, Yahoo! and Google do not have MBAs (in fact, you will find some college drop outs to be more successful entrepreneurs than Harvard graduates).

This is not to say that an MBA degree is useless. You will learn business principles and concepts make industry connections, and of course gain confidence by getting in graduate school. It's the knowledge and experience that you gain by going through the process that is potentially valuable (for business endeavors), more than the degree itself.

Myth #8: In my business, I'm the BOSS.

Reality: Again, sorry to break the News, but in your business, you are not the BOSS. It's the customer, stupid. And if you have investors and a board, you will have to be accountable to them. So there's always someone else to answer to.

Myth #9: I won't have any competition.

Reality: Wow, what business are you in? If you have no competition, the most likely reason is that there's no money to be made in the business you have chosen. There are more than six billion people on this planet, and it's very unlikely that not one of them thought of your idea and left a lucrative market niche completely untapped.

So, no competition is not only a myth, but it's a very bad sign for you. In fact, having competition is good. It validates the opportunity and market, and it gives you more opportunities to improve upon what your competition is already doing.

Myth #10: I'll finally have time to do whatever I want — spending time with my family and enjoying life.

Reality: Ask any entrepreneur and they will tell how busy they are juggling many projects and wearing many hats. The fact is there are many personal and financial benefits of having your own business, but also many personal sacrifices. Having plenty of free time is just not high on the list of entrepreneurial realities.

You may have a little more flexibility with your time, but there are still some major sacrifices, such as sleep. Starting up a small business means you are accountable for everything and often that translates into working late nights and weekends if required. Those dreams of taking long vacations while your business grows itself… well, those dreams take a long time to come true.

All these myths can be summarized in one slogan: it's the customer, stupid. Success in business is not about having a brilliant idea. Bright ideas are a dime a dozen. Business is about taking a bright idea and pulling together a team that can turn that idea into a product and bring that product to customers who want to buy it.

It's that simple and yet quite complicated.

The next chapter, **"What It Takes"**, addresses the very critical question: do you have what it takes to quit your job and be successful in business? But first, take this 10 question exercise to find out if you are ready to break the 9 to 5 jail.

❢ Now Take Action #2: Are you ready to break the shackles? ❢

Answer the following ten questions with a yes or no.

Question	Response Y / N
Have you fully evaluated your current situation and feel sure that breaking free is the right thing to do now?	
Did you identify with 2 or more excuses and myths discussed in this chapter?	
Have you determined how much you will need to survive for a year without a steady paycheck?	
Do you have a plan to meet your financial obligations during the startup phase?	
Does your spouse, family, or friends support your idea?	
Were you able to come up with some business ideas from the exercises in this chapter?	
Have you identified a target market?	
Have you begun your market research, perhaps with informal focus groups or a questionnaire?	
Do you have a transition plan ready to execute?	
Do you feel emotionally ready to handle a radical shift in your lifestyle?	
Total	

If you answered yes to all of these questions, then you are well on your way. The remainder of this book will help you figure out next steps.

If you answered yes to most of these (6 or more), then you are certainly ready to break the 9 to 5 jail. Depending on which questions you struggled with, you might want to take more time to evaluate your situation so that you can be poised for success when you launch out on your own.

If you answered yes to 5 or fewer of these questions, you may be on your way to breaking free, but it's not yet time for you. Review the lists and suggestions in the chapter and think through these things. This is a tough decision, and it is okay if it's not time – better to be prepared and do well than unprepared and fail miserably.

If you want more information and inspiration to break out of the 9-5 jail and want to join a community of others who are working their way toward freedom, check out www.breakingthe9to5jail.com.

HOW JOHN HARTHORNE, A STRATEGY CONSULTANT, BROKE FREE FROM THE 9 TO 5 JAIL

John Harthrone, founder and CEO of MassChallenge, escaped the corporate world when he combined forces with a co-worker to help others start their entrepreneurships. Here's his story:

Who are you and what kind of corporate job were you at?

I'm John Harthrone, founder and CEO of MassChallenge, a startup accelerator and competition designed to catalyze a startup renaissance by connecting high-impact startups from around the world with the resources they need to launch and succeed. Before co-founding MassChallenge, Akhil Nigam and I were both at Bain and Company. I was mostly doing strategy consulting in the Private Equity Group.

What made you leave the job? When did you realize that you wanted to be an entrepreneur and why?

Launching a startup was always my plan. I would have gone straight to a startup out of school, but I needed to pay down some of my student loans first. The economy was terrible then (Dec. 2008) and that complicated my decision to leave Bain, but I decided to go for it anyway.

What did you do to break the corporate jail? How did you prepare for the employee to entrepreneur transition?

Honestly, I just dove in without any lengthy preparation. I did create a financial buffer by setting aside some cash because I knew I wouldn't make money for a while. Otherwise, Akhil and I just launched a startup and began focusing 100% on getting our idea off the ground.

What is one resource (person, coach, book, organization anything) that helped the most/best?

We went back to our MBA contacts. I had won the MIT 100K and another prize at MIT for entrepreneurship, and I had also run a conference on startups. I circled back to all my favorite contacts and mentors from those activities and vetted our plan for MassChallenge with all of them. Feedback from Ken Morse, Joe Hadzima, Howard Anderson and Desh Deshpande was extremely helpful. Each of them made introductions to even more people, creating a sort of domino effect of support and mentorship. The Microsoft NERD Center runs a lot of great events in Cambridge and provided direct support to us early on as well. The state of Massachusetts and the city of Boston both have very enlightened leadership, and we also received outstanding advice and support from our political leaders.

What do you know now that you wish if only you knew when you made the transition?

I don't think I would have done much differently – jumping in with 100% focus was the right plan. We made some mistakes for sure, but going through that learning process is crucial to any entrepreneur's success.

Any suggestions for aspiring entrepreneurs?

Go for it, and go for a goal that you care about deeply. Keep in mind that the statistics show that your startup probably won't succeed, and so it's a good idea to create a safety net or financial cushion. Then just dive in 100% and let your passion help fuel your success. If you care enough about your goal, you'll power through all of those challenges because you simply won't allow yourself to fail.

How are you doing and how do you feel now?

I am very happy with MassChallenge's progress, but we still have a long way to go before I would call this truly successful. We are trying to do a lot with very few resources, and that can be totally exhausting one day and absolutely exhilarating the next. Every day comes with challenges and opportunities, and the process continues to be rewarding as we keep growing and expanding our possibilities. So, overall I'm very happy, thank you.

Key Takeaway

John Harthrone does not boast of being successful quite yet. To each person, success means something else. Also, each person starts out their business by a different approach. For John, diving in feet first without looking back was his style, and so far, it has worked out well. He utilized past contacts to create a network of mentors, creating stronger ties as he went. Now his business MassChallenge helps others jump into the fray.

CHAPTER 3:
WHAT IT TAKES

"Whether you think you can or you can't, you're right."
– Henry Ford

Now before we go any further, let's talk about what it takes to be an entrepreneur. An entrepreneur in essence is more of a personality than a person. An entrepreneur is a very unique mix of a businessman, a leader, an investor, a partner, a spouse, a friend, a client, a staff, a janitor, a manager, a mentor, a novice, everything at the same time. The most important characteristic of an entrepreneur is the ability to switch from one role to another almost instantly and seamlessly. Just the way a chameleon changes color based on situation, fear, surroundings, temperature, and their mood, a successful entrepreneur excels at juggling roles based on situation and necessity. And as an aspiring entrepreneur, you need to understand the importance of this characteristic and develop this skill of adaptability.

Let's take a look at some of the absolutely necessary skills and traits of seasoned entrepreneurs:

Entrepreneur

Self Confidence	Curiosity	Risk Tolerance	Stable
Common Sense	Creativity	Doer	Leadership
Business Savvy	Expertise	Visionary	Jack of All

ℹ Self Confidence: Successful entrepreneurs are full of confidence. They have full faith in their business, their team, and most importantly themselves.

ℹ High Risk Tolerance: Entrepreneurs are not afraid to take risks, and they understand the principle of no risk no reward very well.

ℹ Doer (and not just a Dreamer): A real entrepreneur knows how to roll up his sleeves and get busy making his dreams come true.

ℹ Curious: Entrepreneurs are curious by nature. They have this hunger to know it all. They may not want to master everything, but they certainly do want to have a good understanding over the matter.

- Common sense: Entrepreneurs are street smart. They have to make the best decisions possible in the least amount of time and usually with few resources. They need to act. Common sense empowers them to act quickly and confidently.

- Vision: A vision is the ability to see what others cannot see. The ability of having a picture in your mind of exactly the result you intend to produce gives the visionary entrepreneur the ability to see exactly what his or her business is going to look like in every detail.

- Expertise: Most entrepreneurs are masters of their own domains. In fact the most important reason behind their success is that they are among the best at what they do.

- Business Savvy: Entrepreneurs are not just good at their own domain; they have great business acumen, which helps them build a solid business in their domain.

- Emotional Stability: Entrepreneurs are very stable emotionally and know how to handle the ups and downs that come with business and the risks associated.

- Creative: Entrepreneurs are creative; they do not just think out of the box, they live and breathe outside the box (read cubicle). They practice innovation in everything they do.

- Leadership: Entrepreneurs are great leaders. They know where they are going, and most importantly, they know how to get others to follow and help them get there.

- Jack of All: This is the most important one. Most successful entrepreneurs are jack of all trades. They can fit into different roles as needed, they can wear many hats, and they can juggle many balls. And, they are good at it.

How do you measure up? Take a look at your list of pros and cons from your current job and then review the list of successful entrepreneurial traits. Do you see yourself in these characteristics? Take time to analyze how the two relate. For instance, perhaps in your list of pros and cons with your 9 to 5 job you listed that you are frustrated that your ideas are ignored. Well, it sounds like you are a "Doer" and you are "Creative," but you have just been stifled by your boss!

Now, let's take a closer look at you and your situation:

Each one of us is unique, so are our situations. Hence there is no 'one size fits all' strategy for breaking the 9 to 5 jail. You have to do some self-assessment and strategize your escape accordingly. You have to be honest in the process; if you are not, it will cause you unnecessary troubles in the future, which could have been easily avoided with realistic assessment in the first place. Do not be deluded, accept your weaknesses, and take notes on areas where you struggle. Always be willing to seek ways to improve. Take a step by step approach for such an assessment. Chart your course of action and start following it. To perform this self-assessment, you need to find out your YOUtitude.

What is your YOUtitude?

Youtitude is a combination of Finantitude, Aptitude, Personalititude, Attitude, Bizitude, Emotitude, Fortitude, and Balancitude.

Your Youtitude is nothing but a combination of your Finantitude, Aptitude, Personalititude, Attitude, Bizitude, Emotitude, Fortitude, and last, but the most important, your Balancitude. Let's take a look at each one:

Your Finantitude: What's your financial situation like? Look at your debts, savings, bills, mortgage, insurance, tuition, emergency funds, and everything in between to find out how ready you are to start a business and what your financial plan should be.

ᛘ Your Aptitude: What do you bring to the table? Evaluate your technical skills, marketing skills, communication skills, and management skills. Based on your findings, make an aptitude plan to learn new skills and find complementing partnerships, etc.

ᛘ Your Personalititude: Do you have an entrepreneurial personality? Patience, persistence, hard work, and a knack for handling risks are some of the very common traits of an entrepreneur. Now, these are some traits that you can start practicing and building up in your personality if you do not have them already.

ᛘ Your Attitude: Do you have the right attitude? Are you considering entrepreneurship because of those unrealistic big-money-overnight type expectations? Think again and consider the hard work and sleepless nights every entrepreneur goes through to build a business. A realistic optimism, desire to succeed, an appetite to be different, or making the world a better place are the reasons that should be driving you. If not, you need a reality check.

ᛘ Your Bizitude: Your business acumen, ability, and willingness to work on ideas and framing concepts and giving shape to those concepts, the ability to make profitable and quick business decisions, the ability to be a "jack of all trades and master of many," and most importantly your love for business and not just your idea or company, because business is more than the idea.

ᛘ Your Emotitude: Your emotional stability and strength, willingness to accept a challenge, understanding a situation and acting accordingly, control over your emotions (be it anxiety before the big presentation or disappointment after a rejection from investors). You need to understand the power of emotions and channel them in a way they help you and your business.

ᛉ Your Fortitude: Your overall guts and strength of mind that allows you to endure pain or adversity with courage. Your courage to face those who ridicule or laugh at your idea, your courage to accept failures, learn from it and make a bigger, better comeback, because that's the heart of entrepreneurship.

ᛉ Your Balancitude: This is very important because this is your ability to balance everything you have: family, friends, kids, relatives, dreams, emotions, money, staff, business, customers, new ideas, partners, competitors, affiliates, and the list can go on forever... Organizing, planning, and executing can help you get started, and in very little time you will have a great balancitude.

So, determine your Youtitude before planning your exit from the cubicle. You may have all, none, some, one, or fractions of the above, and that's alright. Our lives, personalities, background, situations, ideas... everything is unique in its own way. Therefore, you need to find your unique Youtitude and start crafting a strategy to escape the 9 to 5 jail. Use a chart like this one:

YOUtitude	Struggle	Solutions	Action	Follow-up
Finantitude				
Aptitude				
Personalititude				
Attitude				
Bizitude				
Emotitude				
Fortitude				
Balancitude				

For instance, you might identify, "Hey, I do not know anything about marketing," under your Aptitude struggles. Well then, make sure your escape plan has some solutions, such as reading Marketing 101 books, taking a marketing class, seeking help from a marketing coach, hiring a marketing manager, partnering with someone who has marketing experience, or even outsourcing the whole function to a marketing service provider. Add an action step, which is nothing but the option(s) you choose to practice, from the possible solutions. Do not forget to add a follow-up step, it could be a deadline to look back into this subject or a reflection/ accountability meet.

Before we move on, let me tell you that even the most successful entrepreneurs are not perfect with all of their _____titudes, so do not let struggle areas disappoint you. In fact, you should feel more confident because now you know what the problem areas are and how to work around them. Plus, you can always hire or seek occasional help to fill in some of these needs and gaps. Now, it's important to understand that there are issues that you can address by hiring others; however, there are many issues that you can not just hire someone to take care of for you. For example, you cannot hire someone to be patient or persistent on your behalf. So, understand your struggle areas to find the best suited solutions.

Leadership is another one of those critical areas. Remember, no matter how many people are involved in, working with, and managing your business, you should be the source of leadership and direction for all those helping you. As an entrepreneur, you have to be a leader and make sure the business is headed the right direction.

Here's a list of questions (not in any order) that you can use for the Youtitude assessment:

- What's my financial situation like?
- How I will pay the bills?
- Am I ready to start a business of my own?
- Is my spouse ready?
- How much money do I need to start my business?
- How I will manage/seek initial investment?
- What do I bring on the table?

- Do I have an entrepreneurial personality?
- What types of people do I like working with?
- Am I here for a get-rich-quick scheme, the BIG overnight money?
- What are my business skills and strengths?
- Am I emotionally stable and strong?
- Do I have the courage?
- What is my risk tolerance level?
- Am I easily discouraged by criticism and/or failures?
- How I will balance work-life-business?
- What if the business does not work out?

This list is just to get your thoughts and assessment rolling; I would highly recommend addressing this assessment with your own questions so that your assessment is as unique as your situation and the solutions are tailored to you.

Are You Ready to Take the Leap?

Before making the big decision, the most important part is your emotional and mental readiness. Confidence is a state of mind. And that confidence comes from the knowledge of both your strengths and your weaknesses. Self-confidence gives someone a belief in his or her own resources and abilities, makes them proud of themself. Someone who has self-confidence knows their value and is optimistic about their ability to achieve. You need to consider these questions and doubts and address each one sincerely – be optimistic, but be realistic.

As an employee, you have been used to the lifestyle of 9 to 5 work hours, set and limited responsibilities, steady paychecks each month, and a few hours for friends and family. An entrepreneur, on the other hand, does work outside the 9 to 5 window, is responsible for everything in the business, and most importantly, there is no such thing as a monthly paycheck for them. An entrepreneur gets paid when the business does well, unlike an employee who does get a paycheck regardless of profitability. Point is, since you are starting out in business, you might not get a lot of time for friends and family in the initial year(s). You might not earn as much as your salary during the first few months of your business, and you might find yourself working at odd hours. If your business picks up from day one, you might find that you are earning more than what you did at your day job, but you will be working more than you were at your job as well. So, be ready for this big change in lifestyle.

Mental Readiness means that you have thought through the challenges and decided to take the leap. Your mental readiness is directly proportional to:

- Your desire to achieve: Do you have a burning desire to progress, excel, perform, and succeed?

- Your power appeal: Do you like to control or being controlled?

- Your ambitions: Do you constantly look for ways to take on difficult projects, to achieve your dreams?

- Your freedom: Do you want to be your own boss and be able to make your own choices independently?

- Your perseverance: Do you have the constant determination to find solutions to problems?

- Your self-confidence: Do you believe in yourself?

- Your tolerance toward ambiguity: Can you tolerate ambiguity, and handle the stress created by uncertainty?

- Your perception to act upon your destiny: Do you attribute success to luck or work?

Factored together, your Youtitude and Mental Readiness determines how ready you are for the employee to entrepreneur transition. Generally speaking, the fewer the struggle areas in Youtitude assessment and the higher the positive responses to the Mental

Readiness items above, the more ready you are for the entrepreneurial plunge. However, more struggle areas on Youtitude assessment or anxiety on the Mental Readiness items do not mean that you cannot be an entrepreneur; they just help you identify the critical areas that need extra work and attention before the jump.

Work Harder and Smarter

Remember, it takes a lot of hard work to establish a business. Most of the time, you have to work harder than what you are used to in a day job. The initial years are always hard. You have to consider this and willingly accept the sacrifices required to establish it. You need to work harder and smarter. The smarter you act, the better the chances of succeeding in less time. And remember, smart does not necessarily mean you need a college degree or an MBA; it means you need to develop and sharpen your business acumen. Smarter means you have to be smart enough not to waste time and keep yourself focused on the challenge at hand; it means you are aware of what's happening in the business environment and prepare accordingly; it means you may not know all the answers, but you know how and where to look for them.

Do not start with very high expectations. And that does not mean you should not dream big. It means that you should not count on your sales forecast to pay your mortgage and other bills. In the first few months, many businesses do not make enough to pay the business expenses, let alone profits. So, be realistic and be prepared.

Success is never guaranteed, and the variables and factors can sometimes be out of your control. But if you ask yourself honestly, before taking the plunge, "Do I have what it takes to run a business?" The answer should tell you if the "American Dream" is right for you. Because whether you think you can or you cannot, you are right either way.

¶ Now Take Action! #3: Do I Have What It Takes? ¶

Take a moment to consider if this path is really something for you. Simply hating your job may not be enough of a reason to step out on your own. Use the questions below to evaluate your current position again, now that you've read this chapter.

- ¶ Write down all projects that you have started in past 5 years, and their completion/ success statuses? This can be anything from small projects to huge undertakings.

- ¶ For each one that you quit or did not finish, write down the reasons why. Was it difficulty, no time, not profitable, no passion about it, or did you only tried it to get rich quick?

- ¶ Evaluate your reasons of giving up and get to the bottom of why and if you'll have similar problem in the new venture (losing interest after a while, no time, etc.)

This is a pivotal moment for you. If you don't seriously consider the types of issues you might face, you may find yourself repeating the same mistakes over and over again. Just because you have a good idea, that doesn't mean you're the right person for it, and that doesn't mean it's the great idea you need to motivate yourself to actually make it happen. If you don't work on those critical areas by identifying them and possible solutions, then you can't expect yourself to grow into it...

HOW BHAVIN PARIKH WENT FROM CONSULTANT TO ENTREPRENEUR

While the perks of a corporate job were worthwhile to him, Bhavin Parikh decided the challenges and successes of owning his own business was what he really wanted. Let's learn how he escaped the 9 to 5 jail and how he's doing now.

Who are you and what kind of corporate job were you at?

I'm Bhavin Parikh. After I graduated college, I went to work for Deloitte Consulting in their technology practice. Consulting definitely had its perks- airline miles, hotel points and free dinners! I also enjoyed my day-to-day work, working with clients and solving a wide array of problems from improving basic processes to building technological systems.

What made you leave the job? When did you realize that you wanted to be an entrepreneur and why?

After 5 years of consulting, the travel and work began to wear on me. I found myself constantly working on side projects, such as a personal finance database that automatically reconciled my manual entry of all expenses against a spreadsheet I downloaded from my AMEX card (yes, I am a nerd and this was pre-Mint). I dreamed about turning these projects into businesses but didn't know how or where to start. So, what does a tired, entrepreneurial-minded consultant do? Go to business school!

What did you do to break the corporate jail? How did you prepare for the employee to entrepreneur transition?

In many ways, going to business school was a copout. I really wanted to be an entrepreneur, but I didn't have the guts to take the leap. Business school eased the transition. I was fortunate enough to get into the Haas School of Business at UC Berkeley (go bears!), which put me in the heart of Silicon Valley. I met an amazing group of classmates, many of whom shared my entrepreneurial drive and also met my co-founder at Haas. The school also provided me with an amazing support system to incubate and develop an idea into a real business. And, because I was working on an online test prep service for exams such as the GMAT, I also had access to hundreds of beta testers. By the time graduation came around, deciding to pursue my business full-time was a no-brainer.

What is one resource (person, coach, book, organization anything) that helped the most/best?

Rework by 37Signals taught me how to let go of my inner perfectionist and focus on getting things done. We bought copies for all of our employees and interns.

What do you know now that you wish if only you knew when you made the transition?

How much fun this is! Don't get me wrong, being an entrepreneur is hard work. I live and breathe my business. The ups and downs are brutal. But I've never had so much fun coming to work every day. I get to work with an amazing group of people, solving real problems. Had I known how much fun entrepreneurship is, I likely would have taken the leap earlier.

Any suggestions for aspiring entrepreneurs?

Just do it. Entrepreneurship is 10% idea and 90% execution. The only way you'll really learn if your business is viable is by taking action, making mistakes, getting up and trying again.

How are you doing and how do you feel now?

Magoosh is doing well; revenue and customers are growing month by month. We've seen incredible improvements from students who've used our online product for the GMAT, GRE and SAT. But we still have a lot we'd like to accomplish, and success takes time. Online video is fundamentally changing students' ability to access high-quality educational content, and we want to help spear-head that change. At a personal level, I've never been happier. I have an amazingly supportive wife, family, and group of friends. My co-founder is one of the strongest individuals I've ever met. I have absolutely no regrets about my decision to be an entrepreneur and don't think I'll ever go back to the 9 to 5 jail.

Key Takeaway

Escape is possible! Bhavin Parikh has broken out of the 9 to 5 jail and you can too. The only way you will ever know if you can succeed is to get out there and try! Bhavin took the time to go back to school and learn what needed to be done. Finding the key to his inner happiness, Bhavin has more fun now than he did in the corporate world despite the ups and downs of owning his own business. If you are tired of living the 9 to 5 life, take to heart Bhavin's story.

CHAPTER 4:
BEFORE YOU BREAK AWAY

"What would you attempt to do if you knew you could not fail?"
– Dr. Robert Schuller

Evaluate your situation

If you have decided to leave your 9 to 5 job, you seriously need to plan your exit. The plan should be carefully crafted and more importantly executed. The first questions you ask yourself before deciding to leave your job are: What is my current financial situation? Do I have debts to pay back? Do I have a sick family member with regular medical needs? Do I have enough money to pay my bills until the business starts bringing some cash in the house?

If you are going to bungee jump or skydive, would you not check your gear, get safety tips, and be prepared for the worst?

There will be problems, and there will be pitfalls. You need to understand your finances before venturing into cold entrepreneurial waters. Truth is that starting a business is not as simple and easy as the media makes it seem like. You need time, a plan, investment, a decent team, and many more elements that help you convert an idea into a sustainable business. So think about the problems you might face if you leave your job to start a business. If you identify the possible obstacles before you start a business, you will not only be able to address them more effectively, but also avoid many unpleasant surprises.

If you do plan ahead and prepare, you will be more likely to succeed. Think about it, if you are going to bungee jump or skydive, would you not check your gear, get safety tips, and be prepared for the worst? Of course you will! Then why not treat your entrepreneurial plunge the same way? Find out more about your options, do's and don'ts, and a plan B.

First things first, you need to find a profitable idea by rigorously testing out the many "wonderful" ideas you are flirting with! Do it while you are employed. Second would be deciding on your survival model – will you flip burgers and work on your startup? Will you take a part-time job while you build your startup? Will you help another startup to make some money while you work on yours as well (learning benefit)? Will you start your business as a side hustle while you keep your day job? Point is "burn the ship and bridges" is a romantic notion of walking away from the 9 to 5 jail; however, you have to be careful about a lot of unromantic stuff in building a business before you get to that startup romance.

Once you know the idea you will be working on and have a clear understanding of your survival model, you are ready to take the leap. However, in many cases you find out the problems you may run into, and it is always a good idea to resolve those issues before the big jump. For example, while working on finding the idea, your survival model, and possible obstacles, you may realize that you have more responsibilities, like an ill family member that needs your constant support and care, or you have kids who are going to college next year.

Before You Turn in Your Notice and Take the Plunge

Cash Reserve

I have mentioned it many times already and cannot emphasize enough, SAVE. Build a cash reserve. Save for the rainy day, save for the shiny day. Make a schedule of investment required and a budget for monthly and incidental expenses, or hire an accountant to do that for you. Better yet, ask for a favor from an accountant friend to help you with the financial projections (investment and ongoing expenses) for your startup. Add your monthly expenses and build a cash reserve for at least 12 months' survival.

Emotional Stability

Starting a business brings an avalanche of emotional tides. You feel happy about breaking the shackles and starting as a free man who owns his or her own destiny. At the same time, there are fears: fear of losing money, fear of failed business, fear of high overhead costs, and the most drastic is the fear of the unknown. You'll never know what will happen in the coming days, weeks, months, or years since the circumstances can change anytime.

There are lots of things to consider right here. If you fear losing money and making a mess out of your business, you should sit down and ponder the risks and benefits involved in a business. Write down the fears you have and address each one of them on a separate piece of paper. Dr. Wayne Dyer (author of *Excuses Begone*) suggests for each fear you have, ask yourself: "Is it true?" and "Is the opposite possible?"

For example, you fear that if your business fails to earn back your investment, you will be broke! Answer this fear by doing a risk analysis. How much risk is involved in the business you are about to start? How much money are you putting in as capital or seed investment? Analyze each item on capital schedule and see if there are items you could possibly get for less or do completely without. Save some of the investment before you even put money in your business. A thorough risk analysis will help you make an informed decision on how much risk is involved and if you can take that risk.

Another way to overcome this fear is to have a Plan B! For example, if your business fails, how will you recoup your investment? What could you do with same resources to make your money back? Consider multiple failure scenarios and creating a Plan B for each so you do not lose your shirt!

All of these analyses and plans should be part of the business plan you need to write.

Mental Preparedness

If you are reading this book, this means you are already preparing yourself mentally to make a calculated jump and secure your future. Even the best businessmen are gripped with confusion when it comes to making decisions. You should be mentally prepared to face unseen and unknown circumstances. You should be mentally prepared to face problems and solve them.

There is no business in the world that does not have problems. The biggest problems arise when you hire a team to manage your business. Remember, the professionals you hired know their job. However, sometimes you might feel like firing the salesman because he is so rude! Try to teach your team the values and mindset you have. Give them the dream and tell them they also own this business, like you. Share the success, and you will have fewer problems.

Mental preparedness also includes determination to succeed. This is the only factor that can make or break your business. We have covered determination in the last chapter, so you can make up your mind and be determined.

If you are not mentally prepared to face obstacles or make business decisions, then you should continue in your 9 to 5 job until you are prepared. There is no way you can succeed if you are not mentally prepared to start a business.

If you do not find yourself ready to take the plunge yet, do not be disappointed, as there are so many pre-startup tasks that you can take care of without leaving your day job:

Skills

Identify what skills would be required for your business to be successful and either learn those skills or start networking with people who have those skills; they can help you later when you need them. Research what all jobs make up your business and spend time on researching these functions. Equip yourself with the basic knowledge of these functions. Remember, as a business owner, you'll be accountable for everything, so it's better to know the ins and outs of your business.

Develop Yourself

Develop yourself as an entrepreneur and as a business owner. Join entrepreneurial clubs and groups to meet more like-minded people. Attend business and self development classes. Hire a coach/ mentor to help stay focused and keep moving toward your ultimate goal.

Business Plan

This is important because a detailed business plan would actually help you identify all the potential issues – be it legal, financial, or conceptual. This gives you the opportunity to think over and make adjustments before moving forward. Better to identify and work on them now than later. A business plan is going to help you think ahead, plan for all contingencies, work with a budget, and keep you focused on your mission. Writing a business plan does not have to be rocket science. A simple, small business startup plan should be concise and action oriented, around 15-20 pages long. Follow the simple outline and approach – *Two Sentence Business Plan*. Find it at www.breakingthe9to5jail.com/TSBP

Help Your Kid Start a Summer Business (Go Play Monopoly with Friends)

Be the investor in your kids' business this summer, take it sincerely, coach the kid, and you'll be surprised how much you would learn from the kid and the overall experience of being an investor. If you are single, go play Monopoly with friends.

Do your Homework

Doing your homework should at least include the following:
- Research your product and services
- Research your potential competition
- Try a few products and services from other providers
- Research and connect with people who can help.
- Start a blog or community for your target market
- Start building your brand.

Now That You Have Decided to Quit Your Day Job

You weren't thinking about just walking out, were you? This is a very common mistake. How would you feel if you could not meet a deadline because someone just got up and left? Remember that one day you could be facing the same situation with one of your own employees. So, even if you have decided to leave your job and start a business, do not ever say or do anything you might regret.

Remember the day you started your job? Most likely you were welcomed with open arms, introduced to co-workers, and supported as you eased into your role. There was an air of excitement and the experience was a positive one. And now it's time to move on. There is a way to leave with the same collegiality and positive atmosphere. There is a way to strengthen bridges rather than burn them behind you.

Focus on building relationships, because it might benefit you in your business in the present as well as the future. You never know when today's boss could be tomorrow's customer or an employee or an angel that will help you start your business just like what happened to Sheilah Etheridge, Owner of SME Management – *'I started my company as a result of an incredible boss. He offered me a partnership in his business but things were not right at the time to partner. He then encouraged me to start my own business and even allowed me to take some of my clients to start off with. The clients wanted to come, but it was a great offer all the same.'*

There comes a time in everyone's life and work when their job is not what it used to be (or perhaps it never was!) So, they have to leave that job. Leaving your job can be a positive transition for everyone involved. You have the power to ensure that leaving your current employer strengthens your relationship and reputation rather than destroying it. So what's the best way to go about quitting? How can you minimize the impact on both your career and your soon-to-be ex-employer? Here are some guidelines:

Give notice: Well, yes, if you can. Most employment contracts require that you give a certain period of notice and you should try to adhere to that. In a lot of cases, your employer may not want you to work during your notice (but you may or may not get paid for it, depending upon your employment contract).

Tell your boss: This is the hardest part of leaving a job for most people. It is hard to face the response of your boss. Whether they say, "Oh, OK then... bye," or "Nooooo! Do not leave!" it is going to be an uncomfortable situation.

Be prepared to discuss your reasons for leaving (even though it may not be necessary). Be realistic, do not expect your boss to turn around and offer you a pay increase and better package. Nine times out of ten, if you quit, you quit. Not only is it unprofessional, but threatening to leave is not the way to get a pay raise! Depending on the type of business you are starting and the relationship you have with your employer, you may be able to negotiate an arrangement to work part time or on a contract basis or maybe even getting some support for your startup.

Plan the transition: Think through what needs to be done and develop a transition plan. If you have pending work, try to finish it. If other departments are relying on you to do their jobs, then it is only professional courtesy to not let them down. Creating a list of pending tasks to complete for your replacement and going over them with your manager is the least you can do. Your employer will appreciate your thoughtfulness. After all, you know your job better than anyone else and your supervisor should welcome ideas on how best to recruit a replacement and transition your work.

Be ready for an emotional avalanche. As with any ending, there is a period of shock and grief. Be prepared for this personally and with your co-workers, supervisor, and colleagues. Remember, everyone expresses emotions differently. One colleague may wish you well, another may discourage you, another may express anger, and another may burst into tears. Even if you are leaving because of difficult circumstances, there will be feelings about your leaving. Take time to listen and talk with your co-workers and supervisor. Their support will make the exit graceful and ease the situation.

Resist complaining: It is best to focus on the positive aspects of your employment during your transition time. Thank the people who hired you and those who mentored and supported you. If you decide to discuss your dissatisfaction with your work, do it in a constructive way and avoid complaining. Save your suggestions for an exit interview with the HR department. If you feel angry and resentful about your employment, and need to vent, consider talking it over with family and friends and avoid venting it out on your manager and colleagues.

Network and communicate: With any transition, marking the ending of a period of employment is important. Allow your co-workers to have a farewell party for you or go to lunch with them. Exchange business cards and contact info. Take time to write to those who have supported you in this period of employment, thank them, and let them know how to contact you after you leave.

Make it easy for your successor: Ideally you want to make it as easy as possible for someone to take over your work. Take a moment and think of the person that will follow you and take over your workload. Organize your files and folder, organize your desk, tie up all loose ends possible, and make your files and notes easy to understand and locate. Make a list of your cases or projects, indicate what is needed next, and suggest a transition plan.

Take time off: Resigning from the job, managing a graceful transition, and mounting mixed feelings about business and future would make this whole situation very stressful. You will need considerable physical, mental, and emotional energy. Make sure you take time to rest and renew your spirit. Allow for a vacation between the two, something like a reboot from employee to entrepreneur.

Start fresh: Forget about your job, your boss, your colleagues, and start fresh at your business. Think about your business, the possibilities, the opportunities, and the whole new world waiting for you. Start with great mental and emotional energy, meet new people, and learn new systems. Celebrate the beginning!

Transition and Preparation

Financial Preparation
It is vital that you prepare yourself financially for the loss of a regular paycheck and the new and potentially overwhelming responsibilities of starting a new business.

Savings
Make sure that you have saved a minimum of six month's expenses. It's always better to have more rather than less savings.

Debt
Make sure that you keep your debt down to zero or very low with a current debt repayment plan. Interest rates are so high now, that the

less debt that you have, the less burden it will be on your new business income.

Business Plan and Budget
Prepare an accurate and detailed business plan and budget. Be sure to ask for professional help if you need it in this area. Providing for yourself and your business is a priority.

Support Team Preparation
It is important to have your support team in place. At the minimum, have a mastermind group set up, plus at least membership in one active networking group online or offline.

Family and Friends Preparation
Make sure that your family is on board with your business vision. Review with them the family budget and any other pertinent information that they need to know, to help understand that, together, they are working with you to build this new business vision.

Current Work Preparation
As much as is possible and appropriate, bring your friends on board from work. Do be respectful of company policies about moonlighting or any other non-competitive agreements that you may have signed. Be professional in all of your dealings at your job; it will serve you well later on, in more ways than one.

New Business Vision and Plan Preparation
Make sure that you have a clear business vision and plan prepared. Remember that your vision and plan will change over time in expected and unexpected ways as you actively work toward bringing it into reality. Be sure to schedule regular reviews of your business plan, so that your goals are always moving you toward your plan rather than away from your plan. Take advantage of your mastermind group, family, and friends as they help support your new and exciting business venture.

If you have the will, there's a way.

When to Quit…

The hardest question that you might be asking yourself now is, "When should I quit?" You may be earning a steady income each month, whether you have a good job or not. At least you get enough money each month to support your family and save some for retirement or kids' college. However, the burning sensation of laboring your life away has urged you to look for the resources that can help you break the shackles and be free.

So, when to quit?

To play it safe, I personally suggest that you start a business while keeping your job. Once the business starts picking up, you can consider leaving your job and be dedicated full time to your business. When starting a business or thinking about starting one, it is wise to keep your day job [read more about the Side Hustle in Chapter 6]. Your day job guarantees you steady income, important benefits like health insurance, and something to fall back on should the business tank. Your new business, on the other hand, offers no guarantees and will most likely yield negative earnings (read investment and spending) for at least the first few months. But sooner or later, the demands of your business are going to surpass the number of hours in a day and eventually you get to the point when it's time to cut the cord.

If you really want to be competitive and give your startup the boost it needs to make an impact, you should start now. Start planning and working toward your startup while keeping your day job, and then go solo when you feel you have gained enough confidence and momentum. Understand that a startup requires a lot of time and energy because you will be wearing all hats – marketing, management, design, R&D, sales, operations, and everything in between. With each passing day, it will become more and more challenging to keep up with both the job and business.

But how do you know when to quit the day job and take the plunge into entrepreneurial waters? This is one of the most perplexing dilemmas for an aspiring entrepreneur.

My answer is "as soon as possible," because I totally believe it's either now or never. However, I totally understand that all of us are unique. Our situations are unique and our decisions will be too. So, how will you decide when it's time to quit the day job and focus on your business full-throttle?

To elaborate on this, let's take a few situations for example:

- You have enough cash reserve to start up and you cannot take the day job anymore

- You do not have enough cash reserve to start up and you cannot take the day job anymore

- You have enough cash reserve but you would rather have the safety net of a steady job

- You do not have enough cash reserve and you need the safety net of a steady job

- You enjoy your job; however, you want to start your business as well

You have enough cash reserve to startup and you cannot take the day job anymore: If you are in this situation, I would highly recommend you ask yourself what is it that you really want to do. Maybe it's not your entrepreneurial aspirations but the current job or environment that would bring career satisfaction. Perhaps you find that you'll be fine in another job or environment.

If it's the entrepreneur within calling, then why haven't you started yet? Go back and refer to previous chapters and exercises. Most importantly, be honest with yourself – is entrepreneurship what you really want or is it just a job issue? Interview for other positions and see if a new position at a new company helps you regain excitement and passion for your professional life.

You do not have cash reserve to start up and you cannot take the job anymore: This is the situation which most of us can relate to. We are so used to of living paycheck to paycheck and have never given sincere thoughts to saving for a better future. We may (or may not) have the million dollar idea, but the main thing standing in our way is our lack of cash. My suggestion is that you start acting now, take baby steps, start documenting and testing your idea. Do some market research. Write a business plan. Write a marketing plan. Start at a small scale, just for practice. Refer to previous chapters and exercises and prepare yourself for the entrepreneurial journey. Start working part time or on a contract basis to pay the bills and bootstrap your business on the side.

You have the cash reserve but you would rather have a job as a safety net: If you are in this situation, my question to you is, "Are you sure you want to be an entrepreneur?" Entrepreneurship is all about understanding, accepting, and taking the underlying risks with the opportunity. Go back and refer to previous chapters and exercises. Most importantly, be honest with yourself – is entrepreneurship what you really want or is it just time for a new hobby?

You do not have the cash reserve and you need the safety net: It's a no brainer, you need the job. You may consider working part time or on a contract basis to pay the bills and bootstrap your business on the side. However, I would highly suggest you keep your day job for at least a year or two. While working, build a cash reserve toward your startup, and prepare yourself for the startup with networking (build contacts, build relationships,) sales experience (if you do not have any), market research, and other such subjects that do not need your fulltime attention and still help you proceed toward your ultimate goal.

You enjoy your job; however, you want to start your business as well: If you are in this situation, you are luckier than many of us. My suggestion is that you start building your business and keep your day job until you absolutely have to leave to support your business fulltime. You also need to learn how to juggle job-business-life – all three at the same time.

The point is that all of us are unique and so are our situations; therefore, our decisions will be too. Do not let your emotions take over your decisions. Think practically and analyze your current situations and needs, then decide the course. Situations may or may not be in your favor today, but you can always keep working toward the big day, as long as you stay committed and keep making an effort. And that's what being an entrepreneur is all about.

Quittin' Time?

So you have made it this far; whether you break the shackles now or sometime down the road, I hope you feel more confident and excited about freedom and the possibilities that lie beyond your current job. You have to weigh the situation and make your own decision. Make sure you feel comfortable and confident about your decision. In the next Chapter, **"Breaking the 9 to 5 Jail,"** I will outline a step by step process of getting out of your 9 to 5 jail, based on years of living my own entrepreneurial adventure and helping hundreds of others along theirs.

⚲ Now Take Action! #4: Get Out of Your Comfort Zone ⚲

Now it's time to break out of your comfort zone. Do you feel ready to put yourself to the test?

⚲ Write out a description of your business or idea on an index card.

⚲ Practice telling friends and family about your idea. Listen to their input and make changes as needed.

⚲ Attend at least one networking event and tell at least five people about your idea. Every city has dozens of networking and entrepreneurial groups with weekly and monthly meetings… so no excuses!

§ Make a one-on-one appointment with at least one person you consider successful in business. Tell him your business idea and ask for honest feedback. Learn from this person's experience and take his advice.

§ Join an online entrepreneurial community, such as breakingthe9to5jail.com, and start sharing your ideas and getting encouragement from others!

Once you start socializing your business, you will find it takes on a life of its own and the momentum starts building. As people respond positively to your idea, you will be further motivated to keep up that momentum.

HOW AARON SCHWARTZ BUILT SOMETHING OF HIS OWN TO BREAK OUT OF THE 9 TO 5 JAIL

As the co-founder of Modify Watches, Aaron Schwartz has a lot to say about starting a successful business. He proves that you can enjoy the corporate world, but that creating your own business has a stigma behind it that is intoxicating.

Who are you and what kind of corporate job were you at?

My name is Aaron Schwartz, and I am the co-founder of Modify Watches (www.modifywatches.com). I worked for Deloitte Consulting in strategy and operations for four years, splitting time between New York and London. Then I went to business school at UC Berkeley's Haas School of Business. I started Modify with a good friend and classmate, Gary Coover, after finishing Haas. I was meant to return to Deloitte, but Modify turned into a business and I have been building the company for nearly two years.

What made you leave the job? When did you realize that you wanted to be an entrepreneur and why?

I loved my time at Deloitte. The people are incredibly smart and fun to work with, and the business challenges that we worked on were intense and interesting. But I have always wanted to "build something." During business school, I worked on a startup which had a small exit. Once I started, it did not matter how great Deloitte was, I had to try my hand at building another company.

What did you do to break the corporate jail? How did you prepare for the employee to entrepreneur transition?

I did two things to move from the corporate world to running Modify. First, I worked really hard to learn as much as possible from colleagues and clients alike. Second, I saved my money, which helped cover my business school and then startup costs; lowering debt (and your risk) is incredibly helpful.

What is one resource (person, coach, book, organization anything) that helped the most/best?

The most useful resource has been a class I took with Steve Blank and Eric Ries while at Haas. They opened my eyes to Customer Development (Blank) and the Lean Startup and Minimum Viable Product (Ries). Our entire company has been built on these principles.

What do you know now that you wish if only you knew when you made the transition?

Build your business from day one so that it can succeed if you disappear. Right now, too much of the business resides on my plate. This is both a risk for the business and also slows down my teammates as they have to rely on me for too many small things.

Any suggestions for aspiring entrepreneurs?

Just start! You may not have the A+ idea necessarily, but you'll learn an incredible amount by just putting your neck out there and working on building something that customers want.

How are you doing and how do you feel now?

I'm loving my life. We have built an incredibly strong team that on a day-to-day basis is building our company. Our customers give us a ton of feedback because they know we will act on it. And I continue to learn every day.

Key Takeaway

The only thing that's better than enjoying what you do is loving what you do. Aaron Schwartz built Modify Watches from the ground up and is working toward having the business be less dependent on him. He wants his business to stand up to the test of time. After all, that is the true sign of success, is it not?

CHAPTER 5:
BREAKING THE 9 TO 5 JAIL

"The way to get started is to quit talking and begin doing."
– Walt Disney

"LET'S TOAST FOR ALL THE MONEY I MADE ON YOUR HARD WORK"

Leaving a steady job and starting your own business is a dream you may have had most of your working life. The idea of being our own boss is so appealing that it has given courage to many people starting out as entrepreneurs. However, that dream is only one element of a long journey; you need to understand the whole process and set your mind to it before jumping on the entrepreneurial bandwagon.

The basics are the same – we want financial security, a great place to call home, and more free time to spend with those we love. Achieving that dream seems difficult at times, especially if you find yourself in a "secure" full-time job that provides you with a steady income and potential for career advancement. While you may have a great business idea, and the drive to be successful as a small business owner, you may be unsure whether it is time to leave your full-time job and start fresh as your own boss.

With every page of this book, you get closer to experiencing freedom! Now we're going to present the four steps you need to take in order to start realizing your entrepreneurial dream.

In Step 1, we're going to tackle the biggest obstacle you have: fear! We'll help you identify the fears standing in your way. In Step 2, we'll show you the importance of planning. You need a plan, or a roadmap, to get you to your destination.

What good is a plan if you do not ever do anything with it? In Step 3, we're taking action and moving forward in your journey. Sometimes, things do not go according to plan, so in Step 4, we'll talk about the need to adjust and keep the momentum.

Step 1: Identifying and Overcoming Fears

Many of us do not take the first step for some reason. It could be family, money, fear of failure, fear of success, lack of knowledge and education, insecurity, plain laziness, or a combination of some or all of these. The whole idea of transiting from a 9 to 5 job to a full-time business is exciting and overwhelming. You have to prepare a lot beforehand, and you need to meticulously review everything before stepping into the world where every mistake translates into dollars lost.

Every business, every entrepreneur, and every person is unique, and so are the situations, so it's impossible to address all. We are going to discuss a few common problems that might arise when you decide to start a business and break the 9 to 5 shackles. For each problem, I list a few solutions that will help you meet the challenge.

I do not want to start a business with a loan or an investment and I do not have enough money to start on my own.

Many of us do not like taking a loan or an investment for the business. Consider the following solutions to this problem:

- Ask friends and family to partner in your business.

- Start saving money, skipping the Starbucks, cooking meals instead of eating out, and many such small tricks that we all know but do not practice. These small amounts will add up.

- Take up an extra part-time job to make more and save money for your business.

- Put you savings in a different bank account than what you use for daily needs and shopping.

- Sell all the extra stuff you have lying around your house to raise capital for your business.

- If you own an extra car or a piece of machinery, consider selling it to raise capital for your business.

- If you cannot take up a part-time job to raise money for your business, ask your spouse to help you out by taking an extra job to raise capital.

- Crowdfund your idea with a campaign on www.kickstarter.com or www.indiegogo.com This is specially a good idea for those who have a physical product like a book, board game, info products, music etc. because you will find your first few paid customers by pre-selling your product on campaign.

I would be unable to manage a job and a business at the same time

It's always difficult to manage a job and a business at the same time. In fact, it is so time consuming that you might find no time to spend with your family or friends. Working a job 9 to 5 and then spending time on your business is always a challenge. Only the most dedicated individuals work this way.

If it is hard for you to leave your job and start a business, and you cannot do both of them together, consider the following solutions:

- Instead of starting a business while in a job, consider doing research and prepare everything before leaving a job and starting a business.

- Ask your friends and family to help you with your business. It is possible for your spouse to run your business while you are working 9 to 5. It is always a good idea to engage your spouse in your business. It can make a lot of things easier, especially when you decide to keep your 9 to 5 job until you starting earning money from your business.

- If you have secured investment for your business, consider hiring an experienced staff to run your business while you are at your 9 to 5 job.

- Take paid or unpaid leave from your job and give time to your business whenever you can.

It is generally a good idea to keep your 9 to 5 job and start a business on the side; however, it certainly is the toughest one when it comes to managing your time and staying motivated at both your job and business.

Everyone experiences fear on a daily basis. Fear is an almost automatic response to change. Moving through fear is the start of transitioning from employee to entrepreneur. The degree of fear tends to fluctuate depending upon your situation. Every new business owner faces the same fears, but each business owner won't deal with those fears in exactly the same way.

Let's look a little more closely at some of the common fears that a new business owner might face. You could be facing a fear of failure or fear of financial loss or anything in between. Think about it, we've all felt fear when doing something for the first time. It's natural for us to be fearful of the unknown. We were fearful of stepping into the pool for the first time. We were fearful of riding our bike or driving a car for the first time. We all felt fear when we did something for the first time. Entrepreneurs and business owners usually feel some fear throughout the business building process. Experiencing fear is part of the human nature. So what do we do when we feel fearful?

All we need to do is take that first BIG step. Remember, how you finally overcame your fear and stepped into the pool, and rode a bike, and sat behind the wheel. Just like that, you need to take the first step, then the next step and the next. Here's how you do it:

Identify

Once you know what your fears are, then you can determine if it is just a passing thought or a genuine fear that needs attention. For example, everyone worries about paying their bills, doing a good job at work, or making a good impression, etc. However, if those negative thoughts keep returning, then it's time to look for ways to change those to more positive thoughts.

Make a List

You need to make a list of your fears. Be honest with yourself. List all of the fears and apprehensions. The more fears you identify, the more you will be confident after addressing them each properly.

Here is an example of a fear list; however, I suggest you make one of your own, because your fears are unique to your situation.

I am fearful of getting into business because:
- I have never started or owned a business.
- I do not have enough funds.
- I do not have a support team.
- I do not have a business idea.
- I do not have the support of my family, etc.
- I do not have a business plan.
- I do not know how to sell anything.
- I do not know how to network.
- I do not have the right equipment.
- I do not have any marketing experience.

Analyze and Challenge Each Fear:

You need to analyze each fear, examining each fear's impact on your business. First, write a list of ideas and solutions to relieve your fear. Write a quick list, no editing allowed, in one or two minutes, and then stop. Then look through the list and cross off anything that is silly, illegal, or something that you could not possibly do. Then choose three solutions out of the list and examine them more closely. If you like, you can write them in the chart form given in Step 3.

> *If you want to conquer fear, do not sit home and think about it. Go out and get busy.*

Look For The Solutions:

You need to list several possible solutions that you could do to relieve or completely erase a specific fear. Brainstorm and discuss several solutions to each one of your fears, and then select the most suitable one for your current situation. Remember that the choice you make may not be the perfect one, but it should be relevant and realistic.

Step 2: Plan:

Each and every one of us is uniquely programmed. No one solution will ever fit all of our situations, and hence we need a unique plan. Our situations, fears, financial situations, business ideas, and every element associated with us and our business needs to be taken into account while planning.

Here's the step by step planning process:
1. Start with end in mind.
2. Understand why
3. Set goals.
4. Write it down and date it.

Start With The End In Mind:

Let me ask you, "What do you want? What is the end result of it all? What is your vision?" Many of us do not get the results we want because we do not know what it is that we actually want. Making efforts without the end in mind is like going on the road without a destination. We might get somewhere, but in most cases we end up getting lost. To get where we want to, we need to first have a clear vision of where it is we're heading. The vision needs to be defined using measurable attributes and a timeline. Once you have a clear vision, you can then set measurable goal for what you want and when you want it and work your way back to identify how and what you should begin with. Also, understand the fact that your vision will change over time, as your needs change, as your business grows, etc. So do not get stuck on building the perfect vision right now. The success lies in having a general idea and start moving and improving. Remember, destination determines the directions.

Understand Why:

Of course, we all want big houses, fancy cars, huge bank balances, vacations, and everything in between and beyond… but do you know the real motivation as to why you want to quit your job? Why do you want to start a business? How will achieving that contribute toward your quality of life? If you do not know, you are better off staying at your job.

Make sure you understand the drive behind your vision of entrepreneurship. If the only motivation is big bucks, think again. List out all the reasons why you want to be a business owner. It's very important that you understand the reason why you are becoming a business owner. This is about building and acknowledging your business vision or dream. Identifying and always keeping this drive in front of you will help you stay motivated during the difficult times that all business owners face.

Set Goals:

You need to set goals to break free from your 9 to 5 jail. Each of these goals needs to be detailed and definite. Include as much detail as possible, like who, what, when and where you want to be by the time you complete that goal.

Here are a few examples:

I need to build a $10K reserve in next 6 months by cutting $500.00 in expenses/month and working a part time job to make up the difference.

I need to improve my marketing skills in the next three months by completing one marketing class per semester at night or on the weekend.

I need to write a one-page working business plan this week to guide my actions for the next month.

So what kind of goals do you need to create? Well, it depends upon your business and your situation. You need to think about your business idea and start setting goals from there. You can also go back to your list of fears and start there. You can create your goals from the solutions that you considered to overcome your fears. Then you choose actions to support those goals.

Make sure you have SMART goals. Here are some examples:

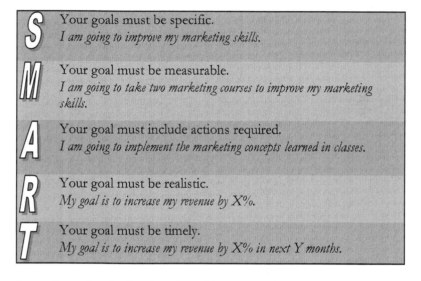

S Your goals must be specific.
I am going to improve my marketing skills.

M Your goal must be measurable.
I am going to take two marketing courses to improve my marketing skills.

A Your goal must include actions required.
I am going to implement the marketing concepts learned in classes.

R Your goal must be realistic.
My goal is to increase my revenue by X%.

T Your goal must be timely.
My goal is to increase my revenue by X% in next Y months.

So, at the end, a SMART goal would sound something like:

My goal is to improve my marketing skills and increase my revenue by X% in next Y months, by taking two marketing courses.

When you create a specific goal, with a deadline, a realistic action to complete, and one that supports your vision, then you complete it – you are building your business! You are moving forward and making consistent progress in building your business. As you continue this process, you will begin to feel more confident and capable and more in control of your business and other parts of your life as well. When you make a smart goal, for whatever reason, it's very easy to reflect on your progress, adjust your goal, and start over the next day or during the next work session. You have no reason to spend time feeling discouraged, because you have a new action plan to complete.

Write It Down and Date It:

Just like goals, your overall plan needs to be SMART too. Do not keep your plan in your head, write it down and date it. Do not let the date bother you too much though; the date is designed to help you move toward meeting your vision. Date is not the vision itself. When you set that date, you give your brain a direction to follow and it starts working toward that date. You can always adjust the date. The most important part of this step is that you have made a commitment and that every time you push the date, it's a personal check on you. Why do you need to push the date? Is it necessary or is it because of your laziness? This personal check will help you stay on track.

Step 3: Take Action:

Action is synonymous with being a business owner. Business owners are always in motion. In order to keep a business running, you do need to be planning your actions most of the time. All vision plans and goals are useless if you do not take any action. So remember, after all is said and planned, what matters the most is what's done. Take the first step and move forward.

Choose One Action Step:
Brainstorm and discuss several actions that you can take to put this fear to rest. You need to list several possible actions that you could complete to relieve or completely erase this specific fear. Choose the best one out of the possible solutions. Remember that the choice you make does not have to be the perfect one, but it should be the best one in the given situation.

Complete the Chart:
Here is a chart that illustrates how this process works for each of your fears. You can complete this chart with the information that you have or will put in each of your lists. As you do this, you can also discuss this with your mentor, friend, or business coach. Remember that you do not have to complete this process alone. It is much better if you can discuss this with someone else. Remember two heads are always better than one!

Fear	Possible Solutions	Action Step
1. I have never started/ owned a business.	- Well, many successful businesses are started by first time entrepreneurs. So, brush this fear off. If you are still worried, take a couple of business courses in the local community college - Partner with someone who has or had a business. - Visit and utilize the help available at the local Government and economic development organizations.	Take two business workshops or courses so that you can learn the basics of running a business.
2. I do not have enough funds.	- Bootstrapping - Outsourcing - Loans from family and friends	Find a second part-time job
3. I do not have a support team	- Friends - Colleagues - Freelancers - Virtual Assistants	Start a small mastermind group of positive friends.
4. I do not have a business idea.	- Write a list of ideas - Talk to a mentor about them - Choose the top three and research them	Brainstorm several ideas with your mastermind group.
5. I do not have the support of my family, etc.	Talk to your spouse and kids and brainstorm ways to include them in your business.	Set up a calendar that includes your spouse and family members in your business.
6. I do not have a business plan.	- Write a one-page business plan for the next thirty days.	Take the first action listed in your business plan.

Fear	Possible Solution	Action Step
7. I do not know how to sell anything.	- Interview some good salespeople	Practice your presentation with a member of your mastermind group.
8. I do not know how to network.	- Join a networking group	Practice networking with your mastermind group.
9. I do not have the right equipment.	- Ask another business owner for some help	Ask for some help from your mastermind group.
10. I do not have marketing experience.	- Ask friends for class suggestions	Choose one class to take.

Remember, inaction breeds doubt and fear. Action breeds confidence and courage. If you want to conquer fear, do not sit home and think about it. Go out and get busy.

Step 4: Adjust:

You are making a change and will need to make many more changes as you go along. Remember that you will be facing changes on a regular basis as you become a business owner. Like everything else in life, change is the only constant in business. Customers, their taste, their needs, the market, the economy, competition, technology, and everything in between changes all the time, so you need to understand the importance of adjustments. Be ready and flexible to adjust your plans, your goals, your deadlines, your spending, and your actions according to the situation.

8 Escapes from 9 to 5 Jail

No matter where you are in your career right now, you are reading this book because you are looking to make a positive change in your life to create a better future for yourself. You may be feeling like you are trapped in a "jail" that feels like a total prison squashing your creativity and potential.

You may be a young professional in a company doing work that you hate, looking for a change into something that is more exciting and/or more fulfilling. Or you may be an executive who has achieved incredible success in a corporate career and is now ready for the second act. Or you could be someone who has willingly or unwillingly been out of work and actively looking to create a career of your own. Or you could be a house wife or stay home dad who wants to start a business to contribute to the family income without sacrificing the freedom and flexibility to be around family. Or you may be a student not really knowing what path you want to take, and are taking the time right now to explore the many options available to you as you begin your new exciting life away from the classroom!

So, let's dive a little deeper to gain insight and clarity to the many options you have that will help you be well on your way to escaping from the 9 to 5 Jail you are in:

Escape Option #1: Change the Jail

Trading your job up or down is the quickest and safest escape from your current 9 to 5 jail. After all it is very possible that the reason you feel imprisoned is because you do not like the culture of the office or the colleagues you work with. There is also a possibility that you do not see much more personal career growth at this company.

To make this escape an easy one, start looking for a job at a higher position or bigger company. You may also want to consider taking a job that is a couple titles lower at a smaller company depending on your career plans and what your reasons for your current career related frustrations are.

Who is This Escape Ideal For?

If you are risk averse this escape is for you. This option is by far one of the safest escapes from a job. If you are someone who can not let go of the "paycheck addiction," this is the escape for you.

Pros:

Safe, calculated, easy to implement, and not time sensitive

Cons and Cautions:

Getting a new job is not really much of an escape. If you are truly an entrepreneur, this is not the "best" option. If this is the second or third job in less than two years, you may want to think about what is making you want to switch jobs so quickly. It would be best to visit a career counselor to figure out what the root of the issue is, so that your next job is more fulfilling and brings you happiness.

Action Steps

Fix your résumé, and start the job search. Be sure to network with the company recruiters and key people in the industry. Also one other beneficial thing to do would be to increase your skills in a specific capacity that will help you be more valuable to the employers you would like to work for.

Escape Option #2: Startup Your Own Business

Have you ever had an idea to start a business? This is your chance to venture out into the big world of entrepreneurship. Starting your company, managing relationships with clients, and serving the market with your products and services is definitely exciting and exhilarating. Making this escape a successful one will not only make you happier, but most importantly you will be positively impacting other people's lives.

Who is This Escape Ideal For?

Those who like taking big risks would be ideal for this escape, as the early days of a startup company involve very little income and a lot of stress. If you aren't willing to deal with the craziness of the startup lifestyle, it would be better that you choose a different escape to help you break free from your jail.

Pros:

Own your domain, 100% control, no boss, unlimited potential

Cons and Cautions:

Even though the thought of owning and running your own business is exciting, it is important to note the failure rate of first time businesses is extremely high. Before you start a company from scratch, it would be best that you have enough money in the bank. This will allow you to live off those funds as you start to grow and build your customer base to help you generate enough revenue to survive.

Depending on what kind of business you start, the upfront capital requirements may vary, so be sure that you can handle the necessary startup costs before you choose this escape.

Action Steps

Focus your idea and figure out what you are going to bring to the market (what you are going to sell). Name your company and create your business entity within the state you live in. Finding a good accountant is a must, and you can also hire a bookkeeper if you want someone else to handle the day to day record keeping. Build the framework and ordering system in the company, and then you are ready to go!

Escape Option #3: Buy an Existing Business

If you want to have your own business, but do not want to deal with the growing pains of a startup, buying an existing business would be the ideal escape for you. When buying a business, you buy the business from the current business owner at a multiple of the net income (in most cases) depending on the industry they are in. You take over all responsibilities that the prior business owner had and start building and growing the business from the point the paperwork is signed!

Who is This Escape Ideal For?

Those who love the excitement of building and growing a business, but who do not want the stresses of growing a startup, would be perfect for this. The beauty with taking over an existing business is

Breaking the 9 to 5 Jail

that the current business owner already has products and services to sell, and an already built in customer base that consumes what the business offers. This escape gives you the freedom to take the business as it is and grow it from that point forward.

Pros

Built in customer base, products already to sell, systems already in place, plug and play ease

Cons and Cautions

Before you ever buy someone else's business, you must take the necessary time to do appropriate due diligence. Find out everything you can about the business before making sure that this is a smart purchase for you. One potential con is that you may be limited in the amount you can change the business due to the previous customer base being used to having things run a certain way. There are definite ways around this challenge, but you must make sure that whatever you, you keep the current customer base happy paying customers!

First Steps

Research specific businesses you may want to go into. Once you figure out the industry you want to check out, search out businesses that are for sale. There are many websites you can use to find specific businesses for sale; www.businessesforsale.com is one place to start! Make sure you have the capital and/or access to capital to purchase the asset before searching, or else you will just be spinning your wheels.

Escape Option #4: Buy a Franchise

Household names like McDonalds, Dunkin Donuts, and Subway are some of the largest franchises in the nation and world. One known escape from your current jail is to buy a franchise and operate it as your own business. The business systems are already set up and in place for you to plug in and start making money from the beginning of your store opening, leveraging the nationwide marketing campaigns each company does during the month.

98

Who is This Escape Ideal For?

If you have access to a ton of capital, and have a high net worth, buying a franchise may be for you if you do not want to buy a current business or deal with the headaches of a startup. You also must like taking risks because, unfortunately, not all franchise owners succeed. You must be willing to work long hours for the first few years, and in most cases be on site most of the time to make sure the operation is running smoothly.

Pros:

Business system has been created, already a successful model, training is provided, support from corporate with marketing

Cons and Cautions:

One drawback about owning a franchise is the high start up cost and ongoing fees to keep your doors open. Without much control over the marketing, you are at the whim of the corporate powers at be to make most of the marketing and product decisions for you. In some instances, you must be present on the property at all times, which defeats the purpose of truly having an asset that grows without you. If you are considering a franchise, just know the rules before signing on the dotted line!

Action Steps:

If you want to run a franchise, the first step is to start researching the potential opportunities. There are various franchise websites for you to do your research on, and Google is going to be your best friend. You can also go to the various franchise websites to find more information on them as you continue your search on building an effective business within the franchising model!

Escape Option #5: Consulting

Going down the consulting route is another escape when looking to get out of your current jail. If you are someone who knows how to do something really well, and are able to manage and help a wide range of clients with your skill, then the consulting route may be an effective way for you to break free. Working one on one with people in many different industries can get tiresome, but it is certainly rewarding when you are able to help people solve their problems and issues.

Who is This Escape Ideal For?

If you are someone who has a lot of experience in a given field, and can effectively package and quantify the value you can bring to an industry and potential clients, this escape may be the ideal one for you. If you are able to handle a little bit of risk, and have a good amount of connections to get started out of the gate, becoming a consultant will become a natural transition in fulfilling your dream of being your own boss. Like a startup, you will have to create everything from scratch, but one benefit to that is everything you choose to do is unique to you as you won't have a boss telling you what to do.

Pros:

No boss, set your own hours, work with many clients, charge high fees.

Cons and Cautions:

One thing you must know as a consultant is that if you cannot effectively quantify what you will be doing for clients, and illustrate how you have helped previous clients in the past, the chance that someone will hire you is slim to none. Be sure that before you jump into the consulting world that you have enough credibility to sell before you start your own consulting business. The fact is people want to deal with people who can promise something and then deliver. If you are out in the marketplace making it seem like you can really help people when you can not, it may do more harm than good to your reputation long term.

Action Steps

Think about what you would like to consult with people on, and then find an effective way to package and sell it. Start leveraging your connections and get everything up and running as soon as possible!

Escape Option #6: Temporary Worker / Freelancer

Very similar to the consulting route, this escape is a consulting business to a lesser degree. If you are someone with a skill, or are only looking for temporary work, any one of the escapes in option number six may be for you. As a temporary worker you are able to work in many different fields on an hourly wage. As a service provider you can provide specific services to the marketplace depending on what niche or industry you choose. As a freelancer you are able to work with the freedom to choose who you work with and what you do for them. Typically as a freelancer the work tends to be inconsistent, so it is your job to keep your marketing pipeline full with potential prospects.

Who is This Escape Ideal For?

If you are someone who is in a transition period in your life, and you aren't sure what you want to do next, any one of these escapes in number six is a viable option. To be able to test and try out various paths as illustrated above is exciting. Just like with a startup, or any other type of business, there are potential risks, but once you overcome the risks, the benefits of succeeding will feel great!

Pros

Be your own boss, choosing who you will work with.

Cons and Cautions

One of the biggest things to keep in mind about the various escapes in this section is that the work tends to be inconsistent. Unless you are able to keep your marketing funnel full with potential clients asking you to do work with them, you are going to struggle. Just be sure that before you jump into this escape that you know what you are bringing to the table, and how you will effectively sell it and make it work right when you start.

Action Steps

Figure out which one you want to do, then take action on getting new clients to work with.

Escape Option #7: Go Back to School

Sometimes going back to school is the best thing you can do to get out of your current jail. Going to school isn't a bad thing if you want to get a new degree to pursue a different industry that you have never ventured into before. Escaping to school will allow you to fine tune your skills, or get new ones to use elsewhere.

Who is This Escape Ideal For?

If you are someone who feels like they have hit a ceiling in their career, or want to completely change career paths, going to school may be a great option for you. More education never hurt anyone, and in fact, it can make you more of an asset to a company you already work for, or more valuable to another company who may want to recruit you. In the end, it really comes down to knowing why you are going back to school, so once you graduate you know what you will be doing with it before you finish the education.

Pros

Fine tune skills, new networking opportunities, experience something new.

Cons and Cautions

Going to school is definitely a hard thing to commit to when you still have to support yourself, especially with a family. Before you make any decision to go back to school, make sure that you have prepared appropriately to make sure you do not run out of money as you try to finish your new degree.

Action Steps

Figure out what you want to go back to school for, and then start researching the specific universities you would like to attend. Once you have found where you would like to go, and what you would like to study, make sure you know when the application deadlines are so that you do not miss your chance of getting into the necessary classes in the fall or spring semester.

Escape Option #8: Social Service

For many of us, it is not about the money or job, but rather about helping others and doing the right thing. Dedicating yourself to organizations and causes to help make the world a better place is what this escape is all about.

Who is This Escape Ideal For?

This is a great move for individuals who have an absolute compassion for people and helping them get a leg up, or helping them deal with their personal issues. If you do not like working with people this escape is not going to be for you.

Pros:

Fulfilling experiences helping individuals, a sense of contribution to society, happiness.

Cons and Cautions:

One thing about the social services industry is that it does not pay very well, so do not expect to make a lot of money if you want this to be your escape path. Living on a social worker's salary is relatively hard with the rising cost of living. But if you are passionate about what you are doing, no matter how much money you are making, this probably does not really matter to you.

Action Steps

Figure out how you want to serve individuals, and then find the specific organizations you can choose to work for to help make this escape a reality for you.

Now What?

Spend time to review and reflect on each of the escape options listed above. No matter where you are in your career, one of the many escapes mentioned above could be your first step toward freedom from the 9 to 5 jail.

While all of them have pros and cons, if you choose something you are passionate about and stick with it, you will achieve the success you are seeking every single time. Do not forget as you choose your next path that you make sure to let your heart guide you, and do not allow other people to make your future choices for you. Life is too short to continually be doing something you do not like doing.

⚲ Now Take Action! #5: Evaluate Fears, Identify Solutions ⚲

If you haven't already, go back to page 97 and make your own table on fears, possible solutions, and action steps on how you're going to deal with them. By better understanding your worries, you can better plan to move forward.

Which of the 8 escapes from the 9 to 5 jail discussed in this chapter do you identify the most with? Or do you have your own ideal escape in mind? Please use the space on next page to put your thoughts on paper – what is your ideal escape and what are the possible pros and cons of this escape route? Use the basic guide below to consider your options.

What's My Escape?

Escape

_____

_____

_____

_____

Pros (what are the benefits of this approach?)

_____

_____

_____

Cons (what would you give up or lose in this escape?)

_____

_____

_____

HOW NANCY NGUYEN LEFT THE STRUCTURE OF SUITS AND TIME CLOCKS

Here is Nancy Nguyen describing her escape from a cubicle jail and steps toward creating Sweet T Salon. Boredom was all she needed to drive her away from the corporate life and push her toward success as an entrepreneur.

Who are you and what kind of corporate job were you at?

Nancy T. Nguyen, MBA. I am a First Generation American trilingual entrepreneur and the author of *The Networking Diary*. After earning a B.A. in Spanish at NC State University, I established my career at the Chicago White Sox and city of Chicago while serving as an Ambassador for DePaul's Graduate School of Business. I've studied business and networked in Japan and Peru. I founded Sweet T Salon in Raleigh, NC. My Southern-focused brand celebrates my Southern roots. She is a lifelong advocate of Locks-of-Love, the SPCA, ArtReach 4 Kids, and Alpha Kappa Psi Co-ed Business Fraternity. Crowned as Ms. Corporate America in 2011, she works to inspire entrepreneurs throughout the world. I was working in HR for the Chicago White Sox then for a commissioner at the city of Chicago.

What made you leave the job? When did you realize that you wanted to be an entrepreneur and why?

Boredom and tired of being in such a structured environment with suits and time clocks. Oh and so many rules! When I'd finish up my projects at work fast, then sit in my cubicle and develop business plans. All the meetings and assignments at work did not satisfy my creative mind and my high energy.

What did you do to break the corporate jail? How did you prepare for the employee to entrepreneur transition?

I saved up money, asked my boss how he liked running his own jeans company prior to his current job, had students at my university conduct market research for my business, then put in my two weeks' notice I set up social media content to allow potential customers to

106

follow my new company, then really focused on creating a community around my business. For a long time, I attended entrepreneurial meetings throughout Chicago to be around like-minded people and asked a lot of questions.

What is one resource (person, coach, book, organization anything) that helped the most/best?

There are so many mentors, but one mentor, David Culver from Mentor Mastermind in Chicago made me read, "Ready, Fire, Aim." At first, I did not want to read it because I was finishing my MBA and did not feel motivated to read another book. THANK GOODNESS I read it because it taught me how to "undo" my MBA and think and act more entrepreneurially.

What do you know now that you wish if only you knew when you made the transition?

I wish I knew about the less expensive ways to build websites, create logos, etc. Sites like Fiver.com have helped a lot. I also wish that I never had a business partner from the get go. It's better to have contracted employees than a business partner when both parties are not able to fund the business equally.

Any suggestions for aspiring entrepreneurs?

Brush up on your negotiation skills, HR management skills, and leadership skills. These are the three areas that you cannot be lazy about. Ask lots of questions because other entrepreneurs can help you. Attend mastermind meetings and visit incubators. ABC: Always be closing. Business cards, ideas, and handshakes don't make a sustainable business. CLOSE. Most importantly, networking. I launched the book "The Networking Diary" to help entrepreneurs build long-term relationships. Without networking, you cannot build a business.

How are you doing and how do you feel now?

Great! My sales and staff at Sweet T Salon have doubled. After crowning the new Ms. Corporate America and debuting "The Networking Diary," I am able to help other entrepreneurs. As a hairstylist, I am able to get instant feedback form my customers. As an MBA, I can think strategically. As an entrepreneur, I can combine all of my passions and create my own career path to help entrepreneurial women worldwide to network with passion and purpose- and look good doing it. My favorite part about being a small business owner is the ability to give back to the community.

Key Takeaway

Nancy Nguyen was suffering in her cubicle jail until she was sick and tired of being bored. The structure of the corporate world didn't suit her style. So, she took on a new style as an entrepreneurial hairstylist. While finishing up her MBA, she realized an MBA was not necessarily the right way to go. How can you tell if you have the right schooling for creating your own business? One way to find out is do what Nancy did: network! She was handed just what she needed at a crucial time in her career change thanks to a mentor.

CHAPTER 6:
THE HUSTLE AND THE LEAP

"Leap, and the net will appear."
– John Burroughs

Behind every success, there are usually many failures

The Side Hustle!

I would never encourage the young and aspiring entrepreneurs to finish early with the day job and spend the rest of the day on their side gig. Do not get me wrong here! Even if we totally ignore the personal ethics, honesty, and integrity part of what's wrong with this scene, to avoid who is right or wrong and what should happen versus what does happen arguments, the idea of using your 9-5 to pay for your startup could be diabolic. Here are a couple of reminders I give to my clients, who want to work a 9 to 5 as well as start something on the side:

ᛦ Read the employee handbook! Well, skip to the sections that talk about employment exclusivity and relationship. Depending on your position, employment contract, company policies, and nature of your side gig – if caught, you may even have to hand over your side gig to your employer, simply because the employer owns whatever your produce/ create in those hours that employer paid you for. In some cases, the contract would clearly state that the compensation is for your exclusivity and comes with certain restrictions like: no business ownership, no part-time jobs or side gigs, etc. You see, if you are not a temp employee paid by the hour, the holidays, vacation, sick time, weekends, etc., all are part of compensation to make sure you are mentally and physically healthy to contribute 100% in those 9-5, 40 hours.

ᛦ They are watching! Most HR and IT have access over almost everything you do behind the gray walls of your 6X6 cubicle. They watch who is doing what, emailing what and to who, browsing what websites, making what calls, etc. Plus, do not forget the office spies, gossip queens, and thin walls. If caught and you were let go because of "misuse/ abuse of company resources," that would be pretty shameful and finding another 9-5 for paying the bills or whatever it is that's keeping you there, would be pretty tough! What would you tell your prospective employers in the interview when they asked why you were let go? Would your former boss still give a reference?

Now, enough of being the bad guy, the naysayer!

I am not here to discourage anyone from getting in the side hustle. In fact, that's one of the safest routes to escaping the 9-5 jail. I've done it, many of former clients did it, and many of my friends and current clients do it. I just wanted to share my thoughts and forewarn every one of possible consequences. So what should the side hustlers do? Let me suggest some tips (and they all pass the integrity test):

- Talk to your boss and get an informal green signal: As difficult as it sounds, this is the easiest and pretty much the only right way in reality. Here's how you do it. First, make sure you pick the right time, maybe a time when you are getting some informal recognition for a job well done, maybe the performance review time, or just a casual coffee break. When would that time be depends on your boss, time of the month/ year (if it's a seasonal business), and most importantly your relationship with your boss. Prepare for the talk, make sure you do not start the talk when you are feeling the urge to simply because you are angry at a peer or frustrated on something done a certain way in the office, because then it only sounds like a rant. Be prepared to answer questions like: Why and how do you have so much time at hand when someone else in similar capacity is complaining about being burdened with work? Why should you be given the special permission? Or what's in it for the company? Be prepared for more tasks assigned from your boss, be prepared to justify why, be prepared to talk about your career and goals, and be prepared to suggest options (you dared to initiate this talk, might as well finish it with a solution instead of bringing it up over and over again). Here are a few suggestions you can make depending on what you think would work with your boss and company (for example, if there's someone in the team or office who's already enjoying any of these arrangements, it gets easier to convince your boss). Assure your boss of the productivity and commitment toward the job and request him/her, if you can have an arrangement of:

- Come early, leave early: How about a 7am-3pm work day, so that you could have some uninterrupted time at work to be productive and most of the evening with a couple of business hours on hand for your startup? This one has the least compromise for the employer and hence is an easy sell.

- Four-day work week: How about 40 hours in 4 days? A weekday off in return for 10 hour long workdays. This gets them the same amount of work from you and gives you one business day along with the weekend to better focus on your side gig.

- Telecommute: How about telecommuting/ work-from home? Promise them the 40 hours and productivity. This will save you the commute time and exhaustion as well as flexibility of taking occasional calls or replying super urgent emails of your startup without feeling the guilt.

- Contractor or part time: If the first three do not work, ask your boss if you could be brought on board as a contractor or part-time employee with less 9-5 physical presence commitment and more deliverable-based commitments.

- If all else fails, you have two options: first, convince your boss that you are fine with his or her decision and keep your eyes and ears open for, "We will pay a lot of money if someone could do '_____' for us." This statement is full of opportunity juice! Can you be that someone who could do this for your employer as a contractor? Second, get a part-time job, with less responsibility and after-work stress, and resign from the current 9-5. Maybe an entry level/ part time position that you know would have least after work stress, so that you still have enough time and energy for your startup. This is a great way of keeping the cash flow in control, working on your startup, and staying social as well.

On a side note, here's what I believe in – rewards are directly proportional to risks and efforts. If you put side gig efforts (evenings, weekends, some stolen hours from 9-5), it always will stay a side gig;

if you do not take the risk to face the uncertainty and give your side hustle a fair shot full-time, it will always remain a side gig. Your call! Do you just enjoy working on one more project along with your job for some extra cash, or is it more than that? Think about it.

Before I answer when to quit, let me talk about two things first. One, let's talk about the life of an individual with a day job, who's running a business on the side, and still has a life (friends, family, and fun); and two, what are the top 5 things you should do if you are considering living this life.

Life when you are working a day job, running a business and still have a life (friends, family and fun):

I believe, for many of us, it's a necessity when starting a business to do so without quitting our day job. It gives us much more financial flexibility to experiment, make mistakes, and test our business ideas out without risking our financial security, but what about the life part? In one word, it's challenging.

Not to scare you, but let me tell you that it can be very challenging to manage the expectations and keep everyone happy (including you). It takes a lot of time, energy, motivation, self-discipline, and support from family and friends to make this journey smooth and achieving this utopia is the biggest challenge. Your job demands 8 to 9 hours per day (or even more sometimes); your business needs at least a few hours per day; your spouse, kids, family and friends demand time; and on top of it all, you need some time for yourself (something I call "sanity break"). Now we all know that there are only 24 hours in a day, and the days aren't getting any longer, which

Rewards are directly proportional to risks and efforts. If you do not give your side hustle a fair shot full-time, it will always remain a side gig.

means you have to fit in more work and responsibility in your already busy (or not so busy) life.

5 things you should do if you are in this situation:

1. Before you even start or invest the first dollar, read the employment contract for your job very carefully. Look for the following:

    ? Does it have a clause that prohibits you from starting your own business?

    ? Are there any requirements such as notifying or seeking employer permission before starting a business?

    ? Does it have a non-compete clause that would prohibit you from starting a business in the same line of business as your employer's?

    ? Many companies have "no moonlighting" clauses, which prevent you from doing any other work, even in your off-hours.

    ? Also, if you signed an Assignment of Invention agreement, the company may have legal claim to any intellectual property you develop while employed, especially if it is related to your current company's business.

If you are not sure what is in the employment agreement on file for you, contact your Human Resources department and request a copy prior to speaking to your supervisor. If you are still unclear after reading the agreement, set up an appointment with a lawyer and seek advice on how to pursue your endeavors further.

2. Take baby steps. Start at a small scale, just to practice.

3. Hire a coach. Ted Vickey, Golf fitness expert, small business consultant, and serial entrepreneur at MyfitnessCaddy, told me: "I found that having a coach was one of the most important investments in my career. I've used Sharon for over 12 years as my coach. She has been my sounding board – giving all sorts of advice from business growth to goal setting, office protocols to relationship building. We talk at least once per month on the phone. Knowing that I have this standing meeting makes me more accountable to myself. And when I stray off the path, Sharon has a unique ability to bring me back to the road of success. You might want to use family, friends, or work colleagues for help, but the truth is that these people often come to us with preconceived ideas and prejudgments about us that can hinder our entrepreneurial growth. A coach comes to us with a blank sheet, an open mind, and the skills to make a difference. They find out what makes us tick, help us to discover what we truly want to change, and then set about helping us to create those changes."

Yes, a coach or a mentor is necessary; after all, we learn better with guidance and encouragement. As much as it is important to make your own decisions and learn from your mistakes, it is equally important to learn how not to waste time on re-inventing the wheel. It is also important to have someone who you can talk and connect with, someone who has genuine interest in your success. That's why we had teachers when we were in school and parents at home. A coach is just the same but with a very independent approach to guiding you, talking you in and out, and helping you make well thought out decisions.

As the world of business moves faster and becomes more competitive, having a business coach is no longer a luxury; it has become a necessity. A coach will guide you down the right path and save you from falling and failing.

4. Be organized, manage your time, and most importantly manage the expectations of those who are important to you. Millions of us started our businesses while still working at our day jobs. It is a common practice and very upcoming trend. Make sure the number of hours that you put into your startup do not burn you out and/or risk your family harmony. And if you are doing it for your family, do not risk losing them by working twice as many hours to get a new business up and running. Do not risk your health, family, and all other things that money cannot buy. Just learn how to balance both your job and your business without hurting either, and you'll soon see the fruits of your labor.

5. Save, save, and save some more. Save for the rainy day, save for the shiny day. You never know if your business will need more investment, or you may get into an emergency or anything in between. So be a smart spender and save as much as you can.

The Leap!

A leap of faith, in its most commonly used meaning, is the act of believing in or accepting something intangible or without empirical evidence.

There's a very romantic notion of quitting the day job – telling your boss to F himself and shove the weekly reports up his you know where and striking out on your own to get rich. Let me tell you: that is not leap of faith; that is stupid.

Taking a leap of faith is about believing in yourself to begin with and then believing in your idea, your skills, your network, and your overall determination to make life and world a lot better for you, yours, and your customers. Leap of faith does not have to be an abrupt and dramatic awakening of some sort where you go to your boss and scream, "I quit!" at the top of your lungs. Leap of faith is an awakening when you realize that life is so much more than a rat race, or mortgage and bill payments. Leap of faith is when you make the decision to take charge versus accepting mediocrity.

Leap of faith is when you embrace all the risks of entrepreneurship and commit to your idea or business whole heartedly. No matter what business you start or how there will be one day when you'd have to take the 'leap of faith,' if you do not eventually take the leap, your idea will remain an idea or a mediocre side gig at its best.

⚲ Now Take Action! #6: Start on a Small Scale ⚲

For this chapter's hands-on exercise, I'm going to encourage you to evaluate the different types of businesses or entrepreneurial undertakings you might be able to start as a side hustle. Make sure to first double check that your company allows this, or you may find yourself in violation of your contract, which could lead to legal troubles.

Once you feel like you're in the clear or have a plan to approach your boss about your side hustle, it's time to consider the many different opportunities you might be able to create for yourself. Hopefully you've already been doing this! Start out by brainstorming several ideas for your side hustle, and try to think of ways that these can be handled on a small scale.

Once you have a list narrowed down, it's a good idea to do some research to decide if this business might actually be worth the investment of time and money. For each idea you're seriously considering, write down the following:

1. What exactly do I plan to offer in terms of services and products? How do I bring this service to one person to start?

2. Who is the customer, and how do they benefit from this? What problem can I solve for these customers that will keep them coming back for more?

3. Size up the competition. Who are they, and how would they affect my business? Don't forget that some competition is good... if no one else is in the same field as your promising startup, chances are that there's a lack of customers! More importantly, what and why aren't they doing that you could set into motion?

4. Consider who your partners could be. Here I'm referring to the other types of businesses and services that could benefit from joining forces with you. If two companies that sell to the same demographic join forces in non-competitive ways, it can benefit everyone, so how does that apply to your idea?

Of course, market research is going to be quite a task for you, even as a small side hustle it's important to make sure that whatever it is you're doing, it's worth the time and effort. While these four basic questions (what do I have, who wants it, who else sells it, and who could help me sell it?), aren't going to tell you if your idea is 100% guaranteed to be profitable, they will help you put into perspective what you would really need to begin working on to make your dreams a reality.

JESSE PUJJI, AN INVESTMENT PROFESSIONAL, WENT AFTER HIS PASSIONS INSTEAD OF STAYING IN THE 9 TO 5 JAIL

Jesse Pujji, co-founder of Ampush Media, found inspiration from his friends, who also happen to be his co-founders, while at college. Now, he's living the good life!

Who are you and what kind of corporate job were you at?

My name is Jesse Pujji and I was born and raised in St. Louis. Growing up, my dad was an entrepreneur, and I think I always knew I'd inherited his entrepreneurial genes. In high school, my brother and I started a little snow-shoveling company and I started organizing DJing gigs. I graduated from the University of Pennsylvania's Wharton School with a dual concentration in finance and entrepreneurship and a second degree in political science. I also met my future Ampush Media co-founders while at Wharton.

After college, I decided I should put in some time at some bigger, well-respected companies. I was a consultant for McKinsey and Company in both New York and Dubai where I focused on internet media and e-commerce. After that, I was an investment professional at Goldman Sachs, making investments at companies in the education, new media and auto industries.

What made you leave the job? When did you realize that you wanted to be an entrepreneur and why?

I left my job at Goldman Sachs because I wanted to be pursuing something that I was both good at and actually passionate about. I felt like I'd put in my time to receive the corporate experience that I'd wanted and was now ready for real entrepreneurship. Growing up and through college, I'd created mini businesses and it finally felt like time for me to do something bigger. It helped that two of my best friends (who I'd always known would become my business partners) were also ready to make the move away from their corporate jobs.

119

What did you do to break the corporate jail? How did you prepare for the employee to entrepreneur transition?

When deciding to leave our corporate jobs and start our own company, my co-founders and I were grateful that we were young and did not have families to support yet. We also knew that we trusted each other and were friends for life. Before we left our corporate jobs, we leveraged resources as much as possible such as big company research capabilities. We also cut costs by moving out of super expensive New York City for slightly more reasonable southern California. Then we cut costs further by moving in with my parents.

We knew that if our company didn't work out, we'd still have lots of options.

We decided to commit to ourselves and to each other that we'd try our hand at entrepreneurship for at least two years. In our corporate jobs, we'd been required to commit two years our programs, so we rationalized that we could give this venture the same timeline. If, after the two years, we wanted to change our course, we'd still be at least as qualified as we were before for business school, another corporate job, etc.

Because we'd made this two-year commitment, we didn't panic whenever things looked gloomy. Instead, we looked toward the longer term rather than just the day to day.

What is one resource (person, coach, book, organization anything) that helped the most/best?

My brother-in-law started his own business and successfully scaled his company while in his 20s. He was an inspiration to me. He provided me lots of valuable advice and resources (including office space) and acted as a sounding board for my ideas.

One of the most important tactics he coached me in was how to take on an action-oriented mindset. I was naturally very analytical, but he encouraged me to actually execute to keep the growth of our company moving. We weren't going to get anywhere by just crunching numbers and making graphs.

What do you know now that you wish if only you knew when you made the transition?

When I made the transition from corporate consultant to entrepreneur, I often did stay too caught up in the numbers and analysis. There was such an emphasis on analysis in my roles at McKinsey and Goldman Sachs that it was hard, at first, to be comfortable taking action and making moves without crunching a lot of numbers first. I was often scared to act until I'd created a model of the potential outcomes, likelihoods, and more. I was experiencing what some term "analysis paralysis." I wish I'd known the importance of execution when starting a business. I had to learn how to "do" and not just think and sometimes even how to do without thinking.

What are your suggestions for aspiring entrepreneurs?

I'd recommend taking the plunge from aspiring entrepreneur to actual entrepreneur. If you have an idea and you want to start a business, get started and just do it. To gain confidence, you should build comfort with your worst-case scenario – it's usually not as bad as you think it is. If you're worried about putting finances on the line, know how much you can afford to lose and then go for it.

How are you doing and how do you feel now?

I feel much more fulfilled now as an entrepreneur than I did in the corporate world because I'm doing something that I love. The nature of my job now is so dynamic. I feel fortunate to have built a company with such great people. As a company, I feel like we've been opportunistic at a lot of the right times and have taken advantage of our good fortune.

Ampush Media recently grew to over thirty employees and we have yet to accept any outside funding. Our first 2.5 years as a company have been a great journey and we plan to keep influencing the online media space. We like to think our biggest successes are yet to come and we're moving forward confidently with our strong, action-oriented team!

Key Takeaway

Jesse Pujji has created a team of friends to build on their dreams of being entrepreneurs. Doing something he loves with friends he loves was his life-long dream and now he's living it! He did whatever it took, including moving in with the folks, to make it happen. Connections through friends and family can help in starting your entrepreneurship. Do you have friends with talents that can help you with your startup? Build your business from the ground up with your friends if they are on board with the idea and vision and have similar passion.

CHAPTER 7:
THE JOURNEY

"Entrepreneurship is living a few years of your life like most people won't so you can spend the rest of your life like most people cant."
— Warren G. Tracy's Student

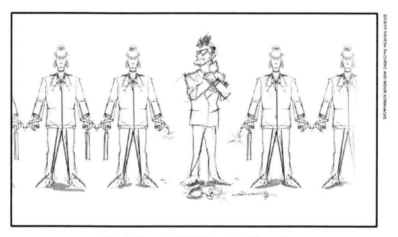

"I'm feeling a tad bit Liberated, fellas ..."

Door 1, Door 2, Door 3

No, no, we are not talking about some game show. We are going to talk about the options you have. We all want to succeed. We all want the best from life. We all want to be wealthy, to have a great house, to travel around the globe. We want family success – a great spouse and healthy kids. Many think that to have all of this you either need to be a genius, or have lots of luck, or rob a bank. In reality, all you need is the power of self-confidence, knowledge, and willingness to make your dreams come true. Knowledge is power, but you must ACT. Knowledge without action is useless. It's like having a recipe for a cake, but not actually making the cake. So to succeed, you need to know what you want, what are your options, and then act on the option you chose to move forward with. So, what are your options? Well, there are three doors:

- Door 1: Forget about Entrepreneurship, stay in the rat race.
- Door 2: Start working on your business part time.
- Door 3: Start working on your business full time.

If you think being an entrepreneur is too much work and is not as easy as you thought it would be, then Door 1 is your option. If you have a hunger to be a successful entrepreneur, but you are still a bit apprehensive about your family and other responsibilities, or may be not sure about your business, head to Door 2. And if you have an absolute love and passion for your business and you can't wait to get started, well there's no better place than Door 3 for you.

What Lies Ahead?

Well, if you chose Door 1, good luck with your job, career and life. You may very well pass this book on to some aspiring entrepreneur you know or sell it on eBay. However, if you chose Door 2 or Door 3, keep reading because what lies ahead is your journey to entrepreneurial success.

Truly said, "A journey of a thousand miles begins with a single step." So, the only way to start is to take the first step. Do not wait for everything to be prefect to start; there is no such thing as a perfect time! Do not over analyze. Planning and analysis without execution has no meaning. Start now with whatever you have. And the first step does not necessarily have to be a business plan; it just has to be an action to get you out of the inertia. Some market research, a blog, a website, a proof of concept, a prototype, a networking group, a vision statement… anything that would help you get a better grip on your idea and help you clear your path to proceed. What's important is not to be stuck because of either analysis paralysis or perfection paralysis.

I'm not suggesting you rush. I'm asking you to stop procrastinating and start acting. Everything needs to be thought through, but in startups, everything is a work-in-progress that evolves with you and your business. The resources you need will come along your way as you work toward your goal.

While there is no shortcut to success, there is a road to success. And we definitely need to find the best route to our destination. Here's my formula:

$$Startcut + Smartcut = Bestcut \text{ (read shortcut)}$$

It's simple, startcut means that you should find the action that will get you out of the inertia and get the ball rolling, and act. Smartcut means do your homework, act professionally, practice due diligence, and work smart and hard. And, this is the only bestcut possible to success.

One Step at a Time

Building a business is like building a house. Every house is built brick by brick. So is a business! Every house needs a strong foundation, so does a business. Ask any successful entrepreneur and they will tell you that it takes lots of work and determination to give shape to the ideas and vision and turn them into successful businesses. You have to build your business one step at a time. You have to be persistent.

A startup is like a newborn, who first moves, turns, flips, and eventually learns to crawl, then walk, and finally RUN! So, it's very important to understand that a business has its own lifecycle and the startup phase is the most challenging phase of all. Even the most promising and profitable businesses take a few months or a year before turning a profit. Of course, we all want to go faster. But do you expect a newborn to run?

So, how to grow and run? Think of it as a marathon. You have to prepare (diet, running, and workout) for the race before running. The secret of running a marathon is preparing for one first, beginning with 5K races. You have to keep acting. You have to keep learning. You have to keep experimenting. With actions, learning, and experimenting, we gain experience and gradually proceed toward success, since we are getting better with every success and even better with every failure.

Action + Experiment = Success or Failure = Learning = Experience

Experience + Action + Experiment = Expertise and Success

So, keep acting, learning, experimenting, and celebrating – not just your success but failures too. Before we move forward, let me tell you a little bit about failures. A failure should motivate you to try one more time instead of pushing you to quit. Not everything you do is going to be a success, so learn to accept and acknowledge failures and make the best use of that experience to turn it into a success next time. Remember, the only difference between losers and winners is that losers quit when they fail, winners fail until they win.

So, What About the Rest of the Steps?

Well, practically speaking, your first step would determine your next step and each next step would determine the consecutive steps. Follow the natural path. Let me explain. Let's say you did some market research on your idea, a complementary next step could be writing a business plan or doing a feasibility study. And, if you started a blog as a first step, so that you could connect with your market and have them support you through the course of startup, writing articles to beef up your blog, asking other experts to interview and link up on your blog would be next complementary step. It is very important to follow a natural path in same direction. Otherwise, you'd end up spending time on different tasks and projects that do not add up together to bring any short term value, which would be discouraging unless you truly know what you are doing and how you'd put all the pieces of the puzzle together at a later point of time.

A not so natural path would be if you started a blog then realized that you need to write a business plan first. So you started writing the business plan and left the blog abandoned thinking, "I would come back to blog once I'm done with the business plan." While writing the business plan, you realized a prototype or proof of concept is more important to prove the feasibility, so you forgot about the business plan and started working on a prototype.

You see the problem with this not so natural path is that nothing is getting done while you are diligently investing time. And gradually, when you do not see any significant progress, you start to get pushed toward the edge where you feel like giving up because you have done everything and nothing seems to work.

Your first step would determine your next step and each next step would determine the consecutive steps. Follow the natural path.

So, follow the natural path after your first step. Identify the follow-up steps, some complementary project or task, something that could leverage your first step, and build upon it. This way you will be making evident progress and therefore more confidence in your startup at every step.

What if I Get Lost?

How can you get to the destination when you do not know your destination? So, you need a destination. You need a map. You need time. You need to take breaks. You need to be patient. You need to be confident. You may get lost or hit a roadblock, but all you need to do is turn back, take another road, and move forward. But you need to keep moving. It's the same thing with the business. There are bumps and jumps, and you may even crash. The key is to keep your eye on the goal and keep moving.

In business, your business plan is your map or a GPS. But that's not enough, even a map or GPS could lead you down the wrong road; there's no GPS system or map in the world to avoid accidents. So what do you do? Well, you watch the road, directions, signs, and surrounding traffic. If you get lost, you make a stop, re-route, and get on your way to your destination.

Similarly, in business, you write and follow the business plan, but you still need to pay attention to industry, economy, competitors, customers, and everything that can influence your business. If you fail or feel lost, you need to stop and reflect on your journey so far, look at what you have done and what went wrong, look at how you can re-route your business from where it is now and move on.

So, Let's Recap:

- Do not wait for the perfect time! Take Action!
- Find the bestcut to success, not the shortcut.
- One step at a time. Follow the natural path.
- Write down your goals. Plan and execute.
- Do not quit. You only fail when you give up.

The Journey

In order to establish a strong business, you need to be willing to keep on working at it. You need to exhibit persistence, determination, and adaptability. You need to view yourself as a winner. Failure happens too easily to many small business owners. It is important that you develop a strong focus on what you are building and a strong support team to back up your efforts in all situations.

Here are some tips on how to do that:

Self-Care:

Self-care is something that you need to be aware of. You need to make sure that you are taking good care of yourself: mentally, physically, spiritually, and in any other ways that you know about. Remember that the health of your business depends upon you. You need to take care of yourself. What does that mean? Keep up with the basics! Take care of your health, your relationships, and your life in general. Strive to keep your life in as much balance as possible, so that building your business does not become your whole focus.

Use your calendar to book regular medical checkups, coaching, visits to the gym, dates with your spouse and kids, and other appointments.

Make sure that you are also scheduling time in for working your business during the day and outside networking or sales appointments.

Think of yourself like your car. How much time do you invest in keeping your car running smoothly, looking nice, etc.? You should be spending at least that much time on yourself and then that same amount of time on your business. That should give you an idea of how much time you need to allocate for self-care.

Support:

Another important aspect of business ownership is support. Where are you finding support? Are you regularly attending networking events? Are you regularly attending a mastermind group? Or working regularly with a coach or mentor for a tune-up?

Education:

Education is another important aspect of business ownership. Are you setting education goals? Do you make time to educate yourself about your industry? Do you make time to educate yourself about your specific business? Are you open to educating yourself about basic business topics? Do you know what you do not know? Are you aware of your personal and professional strengths and weaknesses?

Asking For (Hired) Help and Bartering:

As you build your business you will need to ask for more help, and possibly hire some help. So begin to think about developing goals in this area as well. In the startup phase you can barter for services so that you do not have to do everything yourself. It is important to get to know your business thoroughly as to avoid rather than make the same mistakes that all business owners make at one time or another.

Networking:

The more time that you spend with other business owners who are supportive of you, such as those you find in mastermind groups, classes or networking groups, the stronger you will become. Make sure to surround yourself with people who are on your side. It is important that you actively seek out people who are willing to believe in your business dream and support you in it. Their support role may change over time. They may sometimes be a coach, and at another time be a friend or an advisor. But what is most important is that when you ask them for support, they are ready and willing to help you in whatever way that they can.

Mentors:

Mentors can be business professionals from SCORE, SBA, CYBF, or from referrals in your networking or mastermind groups. Business or life coaches can also be mentors. It is good to choose someone who has more business experience than you do. Depending upon who you work with as a mentor, you can work together for a short or long time or check in on a regular basis for business tune-ups. It's something that you work out with your mentor when you first approach each other. Remember that you may have both informal and formal mentors throughout your business life. Excellent business owners are always learning from one another and from other resources. It's one of the ways that they stay on top of their business game. It's important to invest regular amounts of time in learning about your business because it will yield both long-term and short-term benefits for you.

Time Management

If you are not comfortable using a calendar, then it's time that you started becoming comfortable. You can find some great resources online or you can use a print calendar. Take a look at some of the brands in your local office supply store. It shouldn't take too long to find one that works for you. Keeping yourself and your time organized is an important part of keeping your business healthy.

If building a strong business is your goal, then you do need to schedule and spend regular amounts of time working on building it. For example, if someone wants to lose weight, then they find a way to schedule regular time at the gym, watch their food intake, and follow whatever other good advice they've been given to lose weight. So as a business owner, you need to figure out how you contribute the best to your business first, and then delegate the rest of the responsibilities to other people.

Here are some examples of how you might delegate or outsource some of your other responsibilities:

- You can hire a virtual assistant to complete some of the clerical tasks.

- You can hire a telemarketer to handle telephone marketing for you.

- You can use the local office supply store to finish your print job.

- You can hire a service to place community flyers for your business.

- You can ask your kids to help with stuffing envelopes for a newsletter mailing.

I'm sure that you can come up with some ideas of your own to save time and effort while building your business.

Expectation Management

As a business owner, you have many expectations to juggle. Here is a list of the most common ones: job expectations, client expectations, family expectations, and friend expectations. Once again it is important that you always keep your business vision in your mind and plan your activities around that vision.

Before you agree to meet an expectation, ask yourself, "Will this action help me move toward my business goal? Or will this action move me away from my business goal?" Your answer will help you determine if you need to turn the activity down or make some adjustments and accept the activity. Remember to keep your eyes on your business goal, not on the distractions that are around you.

Job Expectations

Let's talk about job expectations for a bit. Job expectations will be with you while you are transitioning away from your daily job into your new business. They will also be with you as a new business owner. So do not be surprised if you feel a bit frustrated with the amount of work energy you need to put into your daily work. You need to do it in order to set your business in motion and let go of that day job. Prepare yourself for that fact. If you move into this transition knowing that, then the amount of energy that you put into your startup won't seem as overwhelming and over time, it will begin to lessen.

Client Expectations

Remember to communicate to your clients that you are in transition. They do not want to feel as if you are giving them less than your best. So a little explanation, within reason, will help them to be more patient with you. It is important to leave your daily job in good standing, but it is also important that you give your full attention to existing clients and find new clients for your business. You will have to find the correct balance that fits for your business.

Family Expectations

Balance is the key in any discussion of expectations. It is especially important when it comes to your family. You do need to provide for them, but they are also expecting you to provide emotional, spiritual, and other types of support to them too. So be prepared to juggle your time and energy to meet their needs as well as your own. Also, try to involve your family in the transition as much as possible so that they can share in your business vision. As they learn to share in your vision, it will gradually become their vision as well, and their excitement about helping you make it happen will grow.

Friend Expectations

If you let your friends know what you are doing, and especially if they become part of your support team, then they will be less likely to put unrealistic expectations on you, (the same applies to family members). However, they may still give you some resistance because you are changing, and no one really likes it when other people change. It's just not that comfortable. So you will need to adjust once again, and choose which expectations fit with building your business dream and drop or postpone those that do not.

The key is to understand your own priorities, which come from your business vision, and juggle them as well as you can, spend as much time as you can at work, with your clients, your family, friends, and yourself. You will continually have to learn how to say no and say yes in a professional and polite way, with all of your contacts.

Finances

What will you need as you make the transition from depending upon a regular paycheck to establishing cash flow for your new business? Here are some ways that you can provide for yourself and your business during this financial transition:

Emergency funds that are liquid are very helpful when you are starting a new business. However, it is very important that you have enough money to draw upon, so that you do not have to depend solely on your emergency funds. In other words, you need to be financially prepared before you leave your job and start your new business.

Banks are cautious about extending credit to new business owners, depending on many factors, including their business plans and projections. In this case, it's a good idea to find lenders who are more willing to work with business start-ups, who understand their specific needs.

Unsecured loans are available via credit card offers. A word of caution, though, it is too easy to become dependent upon these loans by developing too much debt too quickly. It is much better to limit your use of unsecured loans as much as possible. Remember, too, that when it's time to repay your loan, you may end up repaying more interest than the principal, which will extend your debt payment schedule much longer than you may have planned.

Bootstrapping, or reinvesting your income into the startup business to help the business grow, is another way to fund your new business.

Partnering with someone else is another way to fund your business. Finding a compatible business partner is a more complex process then finding a bartering partner. It is an important relationship that you do not want to rush into. Thorough research and exploration will help you find the right partner(s) for your business. You may also discover that you do not want to work with a business partner. That might be the best choice for your business too.

Consulting as a source of income may work for you. You can consult if you are professional providing a specific service. You can consult as part of your daily job, according to arrangements with your current or ex-employer.

Temporary or contract work is a possible way to supplement money. You can also work on a temporary basis or for a specific contract, again, from your former employer or from a new employer or client.

Babysitting and dog walking or other part time gigs can be a good source of income.

Bartering, you can swap services with other professionals, each person's needs are met, and an opening for further networking and referrals in the future is opened up.

How NOT To Lose Your Momentum?

It's just like Newton's First Law of Motion: the tendency of a body in motion is to keep moving; the tendency of a body at rest is to sit still. In other words, it's a lot less work to keep moving once you have some momentum than it is to start moving from a dead stop.

If we keep moving on our projects every day – stoking that creative fire regularly to keep the flames high – it's infinitely easier to stay focused, make great strides, and blast through the roadblocks that inevitably come up.

Here are a few tips on how to build and maintain momentum:

Interest:
Remember to focus on what interests you. What gives you joy about your business? What excites you about your business? It is very important that you be specific about what makes you happy in your business. Focus on that and develop it. Keep in mind how it feels when you are working in and on your business. Think about it, feel it, see it, hear it, touch it in everything you do.

Determination:
Do not give up. Keep focusing on your business vision. Accept that you made a mistake or feel disappointed, lost a client or experienced a setback, learn from each situation, and then move on.

Persistence:
Do not give up. A combination of determination and persistence will help you stay focused on what you have already accomplished and what's yet to be accomplished.

Keep positive and entrepreneurial company:
When you experience setbacks and mistakes, reach out for help from your networking group and other friends. Make sure to surround

yourself with positive and upbeat people to help you go through the difficult times and help you see the possibilities in the future.

Build a small mastermind group:
Include 3 to 5 entrepreneurs in your group that are committed to supporting, questioning, and motivating one another,

Mentor:
Find a small business advisor, an experienced entrepreneur/mentor or business coach. Schedule some time for monthly business tune-ups and discussion of your business vision and goals.

When you consistently include these activities in your daily, weekly, and monthly business planning, your business and everyone around you will be glad you did!!

Your Dreams are Behind Door Number?

So, which door are you going to choose? Is now that time to act? Have you identified your startcut that will break the inertia and get you moving? Get ready to be free!

♀ Now Take Action! #7: Push the Envelope, Cover All Bases! ♀

Cover all your bases. There is a long list of things you need to do when starting a business, so keep this checklist in mind when you begin to open up shop:

1. Get your company registered
2. Apply for Tax and Employer Identification Numbers.
3. Get business insurance (E&O, Liability, Product, Key Man)
4. Get health insurance
5. Choose office/shop set up. Are you going to work from home, office, or store location?
6. Open a business bank account
7. Set up your record keeping and payroll (if it applies)
8. Get a logo and business card
9. Get a website
10. Befriend accountants, bankers, and lawyers

HOW ARON SCHOENFELD WENT FROM PUBLIC ACCOUNTANT TO ENTREPRENEUR

Aron Schoenfeld, a public accountant turned entrepreneur has some practical advice for those breaking from the corporate jail. It takes time to get off the ground. Let's see how he did it:

Who are you and what kind of corporate job were you at?

My name is Aron Schoenfeld, and I was a public accountant. I went to Queens College, and the only person I knew was a year ahead and an accounting major, so I took all the classes that she took the semester after her. I ended up getting an internship at Arthur Anderson and was the only person in my year with a full-time offer before my senior year. I was on cruise control until Enron happened, but my recruiter at Arthur Anderson brought me with her to a midsize firm on Long Island, NY. After 2 years, I switched to Ernst and Young to get "Big 4" experience and worked there as an auditor in the real estate group for a year and a half.

What made you leave the job? When did you realize that you wanted to be an entrepreneur and why?

About a year into my Ernst and Young career, I was playing darts at a bar in Manhattan, and the guy I was playing against was a composer at Juilliard. He was telling me about this great new type of music production company he wanted to start but needed someone with a business background to help get it started. I immediately said that I was in, not knowing anything about entrepreneurship. The more I go into it, the more I wanted to do it full time. I found accounting, specifically auditing, to be boring and did not like just reviewing historical data to verify it. With my company, I was forced to think and create ideas to grow, which is the opposite of accounting. Once we got our first job writing the new theme package for Good Morning America on ABC News, I knew we had something and had to make a decision if this would be a hobby or if I would take the shot. About a month later, I gave my two weeks' notice.

What did you do to break the corporate jail? How did you prepare for the employee to entrepreneur transition?

The hardest part of breaking the corporate jail was planning for after it. I knew that by going on my own, I needed to save money for rent, food etc. One thing I realized quickly is that most people think they will start getting a salary from their startup in a few months. This is not only not realistic but foolish. Part of breaking the corporate jail is scaling things down in your life to cut costs and prepare to be able to give your startup your all. I set goals and targets that were reachable and met the financial needs that I had with the understanding that if they were not met, I had to go back to corporate America. This served as my guide and motivation to succeed.

What is one resource (person, coach, book, organization anything) that helped the most/best?

Entrepreneur Week (www.entrepreneurweek.net) was a key guide in my jump to entrepreneurship. Gary Whitehill, the founder, became a great friend and sounding board. The lessons learned at the events and connections made helped influence how I went about my startup and allowed me to get to the point that I knew it was a sustainable lifestyle and business.

What do you know now that you wish if only you knew when you made the transition?

That bootstrapping is essential for a startup. When we started, we thought we needed an office and fancy brochures to sell ourselves. After running up $100k in personal debt for an office, conference room and the mailings of fancy marketing materials, we found that people didn't care about that stuff and just wanted to see what we could do. More people wanted to meet at a Starbucks than they did our office. We were forced to dig out of debt and begin bootstrapping after the fact.

Any suggestions for aspiring entrepreneurs?

Use your fear of failure to motivate you to succeed. If you create an atmosphere where you can't afford to fail, you will succeed. Maybe you won't become the next Facebook, but you will create a business that you are proud of. You will work hard because you need to and things will fall in place. Luck is an accumulation of the hard work you put in and this fear of failure will create that atmosphere.

How are you doing and how do you feel now?

I am doing great with my companies, and I have never been happier. Working for yourself is challenging but has a lot of benefits. I wouldn't trade it for the world and am excited to launch my newest company doitinperson.com later this year.

Key Takeaway

One great piece of advice he has for everyone is to let fear of failure drive your motivation. His claim is that with that fear behind you, the rate of success increases. One thing that really stuck out was when he said, "If you create an atmosphere where you can't afford to fail, you will succeed."

YOUR 9 TO 5 ESCAPE STORY

"Screw it, Let's do it!"
– Richard Branson

"I just had a better Idea!"

If you feel trapped in your job, breaking the 9 to 5 jail and starting a business is the best way to secure your future. It is absolutely necessary for you and your family.

This book was an attempt to lay a foundation for you to review and reflect on all aspects and means you have toward leaving the job you hate and starting your own business. Now it's time for you to get up and start your journey toward financial and emotional freedom!

My request: be determined in what you do. Determination is a crucial factor that will help tremendously along the way. In fact, all big businesses that rose to fame and fortune were backed by people who had strong determination to succeed. Without it, you won't last a minute or make it a mile!

Along with determination, you should take guessing out of the equation. Research your market properly and thoroughly; write an effective business plan; do risk analysis and backup plans to pitch an investor; and put yourself on track whenever you step off the path.

Cash is to the business what blood is to the body. A marketing and sales plan is the system that ensures the proper flow of this blood. Without a proper marketing strategy, you will fail miserably. Take time to create a marketing plan; discuss it with people and come up with some unique and innovative strategy that will shock people and urge them to look at your product! Take the example of Apple Inc., Microsoft, KFC, MacDonald's, and all those big companies that rose from nothing and became among the most sought after organizations in the world.

Breaking the 9 to 5 Jail, Step by Step Summary

Not all escape from corporate stories have a happy ending. Yes, it is very important to love and be passionate about what you do. But what's even more critical are survival and success. Nothing will make you money simply because you're passionate about it. You need to build a profitable and sustainable business around that passion, so think of a revenue model. Build a service or product (around your passion) that people need or would pay for. So, marrying your passion with a solid business and revenue model is the key to success.

Passion alone will end up being either a non-profit or a failure. To conclude, I'm detailing all the important points here step by step:

Start It:

As simple as it sounds, this is the biggest step. I do not care how significant or insignificant your start is, all that matters is taking the first step. So go do something – maybe start a group, a website, a business plan, anything... but do something. You will be surprised how just taking a small step will lead you to another that will lead you to another, and before you know it, you are in business.

Understand It:

Understand why you want this business. Understand why you are the best suited for this business. Understand why someone should buy from you and many similar why(s). The understanding of all these why(s) would give a great sense of confidence and clarity in your vision.

Write It:

What's the saying, "I hear, I forget. I see, I remember. I do, I understand". The 'do' in this case is writing. Write your vision, write your goals, and write your activities. Not only will you understand your vision and goals better, these notes will help you plan. Later, these notes will also help you reflect on what you achieved, what you missed, and how to plan around it. Every time you see these notes, make changes based on new ideas and goals, so that you are on top of your game.

Date It:

Simple. Give yourself a deadline and work to meet that deadline. Give yourself a deadline for the day you'll quit your job, let's say in 6 months or 1 year. Now plan your 1 year exit, what all you need to do and accomplish before you quit. Do the same with day to day and other tasks and projects. Give yourself deadlines and stick to it.

Share It:

Share your vision and goals with others. Build an accountability group of entrepreneurs in your area. Hold a monthly or quarterly meeting where each member gives a simple 5-15 minutes update on his business, accomplishments, projects so far, and plans for next month or quarter. This will create a sense of accountability and healthy competition amongst the group members.

Plan It:

Plan your moves. Take one step at a time, start with some market research and networking, and get an idea of the market and industry and plan your moves accordingly. It's always a good idea to make a list of products/services you can provide. Figure out your target market (people and businesses who need these products/services), do some market research (how are they currently fulfilling these needs, at what price, and what are some of their problems with current services?). Now, update your list with all the findings and start researching on how you can solve the problems you identified (once figured out, this could be your USP, unique selling point). Do some time and effort analysis to determine what prices you can offer (do not get into "being the cheapest will bring me all the business!" fallacy). Once you have your target market, services, prices, and USP figured out, you are ready to start putting the pieces together in your business model. All this research and homework will give you clear vision of your business. You'll learn how to position yourself in the market and what direction to move in.

Work It:

Planning and analysis is good, but it's action that counts, so make sure your plans have action steps and then follow the actions steps so that you get the ball rolling and keep it rolling. As an entrepreneur, always be ready to roll up your sleeves and get your hands dirty by doing many things by yourself. Remember, you are responsible for everything.

Adjust It:

Economy, market situations, customer tastes and preferences, rules, regulations, and many other elements that are never constant make it inevitable for an entrepreneur to continuously learn, adapt, and adjust – for successful survival. So, always be on the lookout for what's new and what's changing, because change brings opportunities. If you spot changes, you should be able to spot opportunities birthing out of the change as well.

> *Planning and analysis is good, but it's action that counts, so make sure your plans have action steps.*

Mentor It:

Mentor your business. Sometimes, it helps to look at your business as if it's not yours. Sounds strange? Let me explain. You know how when you go to a restaurant or office or shop and feel "what was the business owner thinking?" Exactly. Give your business and plans an outsider's look so that you can identify the problems a customer would see but as a business owner you have been missing. Mentor your business by pretending someone has come to you with his business asking for advice. What would you tell them they should do differently? Note it down and execute.

Celebrate It:

This is very important. Make sure you enjoy what you are doing. Make sure your team, vendors, suppliers, clients, associates, and everyone involved, in no matter what capacity, is enjoying it. Celebrate every small success, and acknowledge every small failure to reflect on it and learn from it.

Starting a new business or a venture is very exciting for many people, including myself. The sheer joy of creating a product or service and marketing it is absolutely wonderful! However, most people get disappointed after some time, especially when the business is not coming and they are left with little or no money.

Determination and persistence are key! It'll be hard in the beginning, but once you make up your mind about it, it won't be a problem. Taking a business from startup to a successful enterprise is a feat few people can achieve, but they do it with persistence and determination.

Good Luck!!

In the age of information overload, this book is an attempt to simplify the dilemma of a lifetime – Employee or Entrepreneur? Use this book as a stop sign in your life. Look around. Is this what you really want? If not, why are you living like this? This book is an attempt to build a single source of information to help you with the perplexing double thoughts going on in your mind and help you make an educated and well thought decision.

This book would be a success for me, not if it sold a million copies or got listed in NY Times Bestsellers, but if it could help even one aspiring entrepreneur overcome his or her fears and break the 9 to 5 jail. Success on this book would be knowing that it made a difference in that person's life.

I wish you all the best with your ventures, and as a way of saying thank you, I invite you to become a member of the "Breaking The 9 to 5 Jail" community at www.breakingthe9to5jail.com, where you can connect with likeminded entrepreneurs, share ideas, make contacts, read articles and blog posts, and all the entrepreneurial fun you can imagine!

BONUS SECTION:
MORE SUCCESS STORIES

"Do what you feel in your heart to be right, for you'll be criticized anyway ."
— Eleanor Roosevelt

HOW SUSAN STRAYER STAYED CONNECTED WITH HER EMPLOYER UNTIL SHE WAS READY TO BREAK FREE FROM THE 9 TO 5 JAIL

Susan Strayer is proof that an entrepreneur can keep a strong bond with her ex-employer while starting up a new business. Learn how she communicated to stay in the corporate jail until she was ready to break loose.

Who are you and what kind of corporate job were you at?

I'm a brand, talent and careers expert with 12 years of experience in HR and talent acquisition. I was a senior director with Marriott International running their global employer brand and marketing team. I now run a consulting shop, Exaqueo, focused on helping start-up and high-growth businesses create and manage a talent strategy to support rapid growth and meet VC demands (www.exaqueo.com).

What made you leave the job? When did you realize that you wanted to be an entrepreneur and why?

In my experience, as you climb the corporate ladder, the focus becomes less about content, innovation and the great idea, and more about the relationships and politics. I'm good at both but am much more energized when I can focus on achievement, ownership and getting things done. I'd been an entrepreneur before, and the ability to own my own success or failure is powerful motivation. I also appreciate speed to action. Working in a large corporate entity often felt like an exercise in unnecessary patience. I'm really good at what I do, and while I appreciate the support and impact that comes from working with a global multinational, I much prefer a more nimble environment where I can take risks and more quickly know that if they don't work, it's my life on the line.

What did you do to break the corporate jail? How did you prepare for the employee to entrepreneur transition?

I transitioned to a part-time schedule after talking with the organization about a departure that worked for both of us. Sure, it was a risk; they could have said "leave today." But they didn't. Marriott's a respected, ethical organization, and I think they appreciated my openness and interest in ensuring a successful transition. For three months, I worked three days a week so I could transition out of Marriott but also get my own business up and running, setting the foundation and infrastructure. This meant when I separated from Marriott completely, I already had business ready to go. I wasn't starting from scratch.

What is one resource (person, coach, book, organization anything) that helped the most/best?

My fiancé is also an entrepreneur (Peter LaMotte, who runs the curated crowdsourcing agency GeniusRocket). Besides being an amazingly supportive and encouraging partner, he's also really, really good at building relationships and a network from an entrepreneurial perspective. He helped me to think through the quick, strategic relationships I needed and the tools that would help my business get out the gate quickly. Peter also played devil's advocate to me so I didn't jump on an opportunity just because I needed business. He also reminds me that if it doesn't work and I end up with a bank account of $10, I'll be okay.

We're both in this game for the work and the ambition. The financial success will be a pleasant byproduct but it's not why we're here in the first place.

What do you know now that you wish if only you knew when you made the transition?

The importance of long-term forecasting. I have an MBA, but the model I'm operating under right now makes it hard to forecast financials much beyond 1Q out. And that's not tenable for the long-term. I'm working on that.

Any suggestions for aspiring entrepreneurs?

Get your administrative structure up and running fast. You need to have a brand, a site, an accounting system and all that admin stuff ready to go. It can eat up countless hours and time if you're not set up for success in that way.

How are you doing and how do you feel now?

I've found a new spirit. Even though, like most entrepreneurs, I'm working all the time, I also feel like I'm operating at a different elevation where the air is fresher, my energy's doubled, and I'm just happier. I have to balance that with the financial and personal risk I am taking, but I get more done in an hour than most people do all day. I don't mind failing or sucking at something if I can learn from it, fix it, bounce back and be better next time.

Key Takeaway

Amazing! Susan Strayer had the support from her corporate job to help her escape from it! She kept things professional at her job while starting up her new entrepreneurship. Along with having that sense of security while building up her business, Susan also had the help of her entrepreneurial-minded fiancé. You, too, can start your business while still working for your old corporate office. Just be sure to play your cards right so you end on good terms and have a good working relationship with them.

HOW JUSTIN BEEGEL LEFT THE CUBICLE LIFE TO START AN INFOGRAPHICS BUSINESS

Justin Beegel shares the startup of his infographic company with us. His parents' request for him to wait slowed his start, but nothing could hold him back for long. Let's see how he broke out of the cubicle jail and joined the world of entrepreneurship.

Who are you and what kind of corporate job were you at?

My name is Justin Beegel. I started a company three years ago called Infographic World (www.InfographicWorld.com). We are a data visualization and infographic company, working with our clients to create viral content and help them tell their message in a more effective and visual manner. The old way of communicating messages (text heavy, dense, boring), whether it be through articles, reports or documents, is simply not working anymore. Infographics are a more effective approach, as they stimulate the eyes and mind to better understand messages.

Right out of school, I went to work as the social media marketing manager for a large magazine publishing conglomerate. We were the publishers for major worldwide magazines in industries such as auto, fashion, movies and lifestyle. My job was to help with content strategy and to work with the editors of each website to create content that will drive more traffic to our websites and get people to share the content on social media sites.

What made you leave the job? When did you realize that you wanted to be an entrepreneur and why?

I realized early on, perhaps TOO early, that I was simply not made to work for large corporations. There are simply too many ineffective policies and procedures in place; too much bureaucracy. All of this leads to the right thing often not being done because of red tape, and in its place, you end up doing the same thing over and over again, hoping for some new result. On top of that, it seemed like every 3-4 weeks, there was some "fire drill" where people were freaking out

151

because of some number that needs to be hit, and what was being done to get there. It was some fear tactic being used over and over again to the point where I personally just started ignoring it.

I realized I wanted to be an entrepreneur during my last year in school. I had no idea how I was going to get there, but I knew it was what I wanted. Going to work for a huge corporation only cemented the idea. As an entrepreneur, I could work my butt off to benefit myself, as compared to being at some job working my butt off to make the executives money. It just wasn't for me.

What did you do to break the corporate jail? How did you prepare for the employee to entrepreneur transition?

Truthfully, I was presented with an opportunity and ran with it. About 6 months into starting my job, I was approached to do some independent consulting. It was a small job, and at the time, I only really saw it as a way to make a little extra money. A week later, someone else approached me. Very slowly, I began to get referrals, and some word of mouth developed. I was being sought out as a good person to hire for helping websites drive more traffic to their site and help with content creation strategy. I would get hired, then outsource all of the work, taking a small amount for profit, but still turning a profit each time. This built up over time, to the point where I was working at my day job until about 6 p.m., then coming home and working on the side business until about 4 a.m. That was my life for a period of time, and it was absolutely exhausting. I knew that I was going to have to choose one or the other and soon. To me, the choice was obvious: the side work, since I felt I had a real business opportunity. At the end of the day, I was 23 years old with no family to support, no wife, no kids. If there was ever a time to take a chance, that was it. Worst case scenario: the business crashes and burns. So what? I gain an incredible experience and learning scenario, and I'd go get a job or start another business.

So, over time I prepared for the eventual transition. I built up my client list as much as I could so that there was enough money coming in to warrant the transition. I read any book I could on starting your own business and things I might have to know about. I spoke with friends I knew who had started their own business and anyone I possibly could to help me learn more.

The hardest part was breaking it to my family. I actually had intended to quit sooner than I did, but I went home to tell my parents, and as I guess I should have figured, they talked me out of it. My mother and father made some good points, and I decided to forgo it, for the most part. They had asked me to wait another 8-10 months, so I could gain more knowledge and meet more people.

About 3-4 weeks later, I was heading up in the elevator to my job, when I realized I had to do it that day. It was just something I needed to do. So, I went up and put in my notice. It was the most scared I had remembered being in a long time; actually walking in and telling my bosses. To my surprise, they were incredibly supportive and actually happy for me.

What is one resource (person, coach, book, organization anything) that helped the most/best?

I would say the most life-changing moment for me, in this respect, came after reading Robert Kiyosaki's *Rich Dad Poor Dad*. The book had such an impact on me, my brain felt like it was going to explode by the time I was done reading it. I just saw the world in such a new light, and it also just opened the world up to so much opportunity. Honestly, it was so enlightening, it was actually a bit overwhelming. There was so much I wanted to do after reading it, but I had no money to do anything about it. It was only when the opportunity to start my business presented itself that I was able to put some of my ideas/thoughts into action. I ended up re-reading the book three more times, along with several other of Kiyosaki's books.

Outside of that, I would say two people in my life who made my transition from employee to entrepreneur possible were one of my best friends, Alex Friedman, and my father. Alex graduated from college a semester early, and after working for his father a little, he ended up starting his own company, later merging with another company to form what is today a very successful digital marketing firm, Ruckus Marketing. I would pick his brain every single opportunity I could. He was living my life, just simply several steps ahead of the game. He was a lifesaver because he could relate to exactly what I was doing and give me advice that few others could. My father made it possible from a mental standpoint. I would constantly be on the verge of a breakdown because of being overwhelmed with not only things I didn't know, but things I didn't know that I didn't know. He helped me see things I hadn't thought about, and put processes in place to make sure my business could survive. I owe so much to both of them.

What do you know now that you wish if only you knew when you made the transition?

Wow, this is a tough one; tough because I truly know about 10,000 things now that I didn't know before. If it's true that you can only learn by making mistakes, you can call me one of the smarter people in the world at this point because I made just about every mistake one can possibly make while running my business. One thing I think I wish I knew/did differently would be to have more of an education of financial elements. Some of my larger mistakes I made along the way could have easily been avoided with some more fundamental understanding of financial/accounting principles, more specifically relating to receivables, payables, expenses, etc.

Any suggestions for aspiring entrepreneurs?

One major thing that sticks in my mind is to always leave your current job on the best terms possible. When I quit, I told my boss (who was a recent hire) that I would stay as long as he needed me, and I would help the transition in any way I could. Instead of two weeks, I stayed for six. By doing so, I left on great terms and not only was hired by my old company to do consulting work for them, but when my boss left and went to another agency, they hired us to do infographics as well.

The reality is, you truly never know how things will turn out. People leave and switch jobs more frequently now than ever. You never know when someone you work with may end up being someone you cross paths with again in the future in a business capacity.

Another thing: for better or worse, you must understand that your business WILL become your life. As the owner, it becomes something you will think about every second of every day, at least in the beginning (still is for me 3 years later).

Truly understand that you WILL make mistakes; small ones, medium ones, big ones. I promise you, it will happen. Go in understanding this; they will happen. Just learn from them, and try to never make them again. My business was built on mistakes and is now where it is because of those mistakes.

Surround yourself immediately with people smarter than yourself, especially so in areas you are weak. There are simply too many areas to focus on with any business. One person can't do them all. Find the best possible people out there.

Get advice from anyone and everyone. Seek out people who have taken the path you want to take or are currently taking. I also read every book I could find to help.

Find a great lawyer and a great accountant. Both, while costing you money now, will save your butt in the future in more ways than you can imagine.

How are you doing and how do you feel now?

Running a business is one big roller-coaster. The ups and downs can be overwhelming at times, but I love every second of what I'm doing. I always heard it, but it never meant anything while hearing it: "if you love what you do, you'll never work a day in your life." The saying is really true. I never feel like what I'm doing is work. It's because I'm building something from scratch, that is growing and becoming more and more successful, and my hard work is directly benefiting the business and myself. Infographic World is beginning to take off, as infographics as a whole are exploding. People are starting to realize the old way is not working anymore. That's where we come in. I'm three years in, but I know my ride is still just beginning.

Key Takeaway

Justin Beegel had many ups and downs throughout starting his company, but as he said, the business wouldn't be where it is now if it weren't for the mistakes he made and learned from. He made sure to keep his corporate job for a while until they were ready to let him go, creating a bond that came in handy more than once. He made it through the bumps by constant research of the topics he knew little to nothing about. His biggest piece of advice? Never stop looking for advice. If someone knows something you don't, talk to them.

HER CORPORATE JOB WASN'T SO BAD, BUT CAROLINE GHOSN SAW POTENTIAL IN AN ONLINE PROFESSIONAL NETWORK FOR WOMEN

Caroline Ghosn started an online professional network for women after breaking out of the corporate jail. Though there were tough situations, such as leaving her job, she co-founded a business with a life coach who kept things running smoothly.

Who are you and what kind of corporate job were you at?

I am Caroline Ghosn, and I left a consulting role at McKinsey and Company to start, The Levo League, an online professional network for Gen Y women.

What made you leave the job? When did you realize that you wanted to be an entrepreneur and why?

I was happy in my job but left because, ultimately, the potential social impact of the initiative I co-founded was overpowering my current path.

What did you do to break the corporate jail? How did you prepare for the employee to entrepreneur transition?

The toughest thing for me personally in leaving McKinsey was breaking the News to the mentors and advocates who had championed me to move forward within the organization. I made sure to prepare my talking points and take the time to meet with each of these people well in advance of my departure to explain my motivations and get their feedback. In terms of preparation for the transition, I got thrown right into the deep end because coming out of McKinsey I was catapulted into the messy closure of a first initiative I was working on with some former colleagues and then had to immediately reposition my working style to prepare for starting a new venture with one of the founders of that former initiative. It was trial by fire.

What is one resource (person, coach, book, organization anything) that helped the most/best?

My co-founder, Amanda Pouchot! She is very execution-oriented, and is a fantastic life coach. She must have been a guru in another life.

What do you know now that you wish if only you knew when you made the transition?

It will be OK. Sometimes you feel like you carry the weight of the world on your shoulders when you're responsible for a new idea, a new employee, etc.

Any suggestions for aspiring entrepreneurs?

Perfect can be the enemy of good - you want to be excellent (as you should) but startups move so quickly that you don't have time to be in control.

How are you doing and how do you feel now?

I feel fantastic! It is so inspiring to walk into a room full of people who are all dedicated to the vision that used to be a fledgling conversation between yourself and your co-founder in a living room on a Saturday afternoon. Time flies.

Key Takeaway

The old mantra "time flies when you're having fun" applies to Caroline Ghosn's career change. Severing ties can be difficult when you appreciate the help you've received from a mentor, but when breaking out of the 9 to 5 jail, changes must be made. She took the time to make sure that it was the right choice.

HOW JIM GARLAND WENT FROM THE TRUNK OF A CAR TO $3,500,000

Jim Garland is an entrepreneur, business owner, author, professional speaker and business consultant. He started his first company Sharp Details, Inc. literally from the trunk of his car as a boat cleaning service in 1991. Today Sharp Details, Inc provides corporate aircraft cleaning and support services to fortune 100 and 500 companies, has 60 employees and produces $3,500,000 in annual revenue. But guess what? Jim also was an employee once, just like you, so let's talk to him and find out how he broke out of the 9-5 jail?

Tell me who you are and what kind of corporate job were you at?

I am a husband to my wonderful wife (high school sweet heart) and a father to our four great kids. I am an entrepreneur, author, and business consultant. I am the CEO of two companies, Sharp Details, Inc., a private and corporate aircraft cleaning and support company which started in the trunk of my car in 1991, and Garland Communication, LLC, which started in 2009. This second company promotes my book and provides small business consulting and seminars. I held two corporate jobs before moving out on my own. One job was selling office coffee services/supplies and the other was selling medical supplies. I did each for less than a year.

What made you leave the job? When did you realize that you wanted to be an entrepreneur and why?

I left my second corporate job because I could see that if I wanted to succeed on a large scale I would have to dedicate myself to my business venture full time. I also wanted to be in control of my own destiny and the only way this was possible was to go out on my own. I can remember sitting at my desk at my second corporate job, looking at the numbers I produced and then thinking, "There is no way I can do this for 40 more years, I have so much more to offer!" That was the day I gave my notice.

What did you do to break the corporate jail? How were the initial days/months/challenges of the transition?

When I stopped my day job I continued waiting tables at night, something I was already doing for extra income. My thought process was that I could wait tables at night 4-5 times per week and pursue my boat cleaning service during the day. In this way, money was coming in to pay the bills and I wouldn't starve to death. I took the leap of faith; it had to work or I would be stuck waiting tables for the rest of my life!!

What are your Top 5 (or more) tips for employees who want to be entrepreneurs but are hung up on something?

1. Figure out what you are passionate about and find a way to turn that into a business. This way no matter how hard you have to work you will still love it.

2. Start the business while you still have a full time job.

3. Start it from home and on a shoestring so that you have very little capital exposure. Remember Bill Gates started Microsoft in his parent's garage.

4. Plow every penny you make back into the business for the first 12-24 months to give it a good base of cash.

5. BE PATIENT!

6. Read the following books: *Think and Grow Rich* , *The E-Myth, The Secret* and *How To Win Friends and Influence People* . These will guide you along your journey.

How are you now? Are you still in the same business, and how do you feel?

My original business, Barnacle Jim's Boat Service that started in 1991 cleaning boats is now called Sharp Details, Inc. We are a $3,500,000 business with 60 employees from VA to CT and we clean corporate and private jets. I feel great about the business right now and I can see the economy and the private aviation industry start to come back. I have built a company that runs day to day with a management team in place. This has allowed me to spend more time with my wife and four kids and write my first book, The Practical Guide To Exceptional Living ", which is now available on Amazon. I am enjoying my business more now and having more fun than I have had in the last 20 years.

Thank you, Devesh, for having an interest in my story of becoming an entrepreneur. It's great to know there is such an interest out there in what people like me have done with their otherwise boring 9 to 5 lives. Good luck in all you do.

Key Takeaway

It's very important to find your survival model before you quit. Jim decided to wait tables to keep the extra income and as a motivation, "It had to work or I would be stuck waiting tables for the rest of my life!"

Here are a few possibilities: A. you flip burgers and work on your startup; B. you stay in some other part-time job while you build your startup; and C. you help another startup to make money while you work on yours as well (learning benefit).

HOW BONNIE BUOL RUSZCYZYK WENT FROM EMPLOYEE TO ENTREPRENR DESPITE HER HARDSHIPS

Bonnie Buol Ruszczyk is a true hero and my hat goes off to her. Despite all the fears, despite the fact she was uninsurable, and despite the excruciation of losing two newborn sons in less than a week, this is the woman not just pulled her personal life together but fulfilled her long due dream of having her own business. Today, she runs her own company with more business than she can handle.

In this interview, lies the most important lesson that EVERY aspiring entrepreneur must know: *don't give in to fear.* Friends, if Bonnie's interview doesn't motivate you to take the first big leap... then I just don't know what will. Read for yourself...

Who are you and what kind of corporate job were you at?

My name is Bonnie Ruszczyk. I have been in marketing for nearly 20 years now, working in a number of different industries, both on the corporate side and for agencies. My most recent position, prior to starting my company, was as the marketing director for a 100+ person accounting firm in Atlanta.

What made you leave the job? When did you realize that you wanted to be an entrepreneur and why?

I've wanted to have my own firm for many years, but was never in a position to make the leap, for various reasons. I'm virtually uninsurable on my own (Crohn's disease), I needed a consistent income and I let the fear of failure guide my steps. In early June, I was told that my firm was eliminating my position (as well as that of our business development director). I was 20-weeks pregnant with twins at the time. While they were generous with their offer, I was in no position to go look for another job. I felt like now was my time. Sadly, I went into early labor 3 weeks later, and we lost our first son. After a week on bed rest in the hospital, we lost our second son, and I nearly died in the process of the stillbirth. Moments like that can really change your perspective. While I was now, very sadly, in a position to go look for another job, I decided to stick to my guns and start my own company anyway. Life is way too short to play it safe all the time and I wanted to pursue my dream. And hell, the worst that can happen is I fall flat on my face and go look for a new job anyway.

What did you do to break the corporate jail? How did you prepare yourself for the employee to entrepreneur transition?

Once I made the decision, I started getting advice from everyone I knew, especially those in the industry and other entrepreneurs. I was encouraged to proceed. While the economy was still pretty bad, I was told that now is the best time to start a company. Because of my business structure (I'm the only employee but I bring in other freelancers on an as needed basis), I can compete with much larger firms. Yet because my overhead is low, I can charge lower fees yet provide equal or better services as the bigger guys. The last day at my job was mid-August, and by that time I had my website up, my company incorporated, my business cards printed, etc. I went on a two-week vacation to signify the end of a bad summer and the start of a wonderful fall. When we returned, I hit the ground running and haven't stopped since.

What are your tips and suggestions for want-to-be entrepreneurs?

1. Don't give in to fear. You can think of many reasons to not start your own business, but most of them are simply fear. Be positive.

2. Do your research and planning. Talk to others who have done it successfully, even competitors. Get as much information as you can before you start. And create a business and marketing plan for your company too. I think a lot of companies fail because they don't know where they are going, so they don't have a clear idea of how to get there.

3. Pick a niche and stick to it. The other temptation for anyone just starting out is to just take any business that comes your way and try to be everything for everyone. This makes your

marketing efforts incredibly difficult and you end up not being an expert at anything. I focused my company on marketing services for professional service providers (CPAs, attorneys, consultants, etc.). I've stepped outside of that realm a couple of times, but in those cases, I've hired outside help to do most of the work. That way I can truly focus on my niche and create a reputation and brand within that smaller audience.

4.   Network, network, network. I can't even begin to count the number of "business" lunches and coffees I've had in the last six months. But there hasn't been one week where I haven't had at least 3 prospect meetings. Even if the person you are meeting with doesn't turn out to have business, and many won't, they know people, who know people, etc. I'm on 5th and 6th generation meetings now, and it is truly paying off.

How are you now? Are you still in same business, and how do you feel?

I've never been happier. I just celebrated the six month anniversary of my business, and I almost have more work than I can handle. It's a roller coaster of emotion, but it is incredibly exciting and empowering to be in control of my own destiny.

Key Takeaway

Don't give in to fear. You can think of many reasons to not start your own business, but most of them are simply fear. Do not let your fears get the best of you. What do you have to lose? The worst that can happen is you fail and then you try again. *Try* is a small word that can make a big difference. If we try, we only risk failure, but if we don't try, then we ensure failure.

"Twenty years from now you will be more disappointed by the things that you didn't do than by the ones you did do. So throw off the bowlines. Sail away from the safe harbor. Catch the trade winds in your sails. Explore. Dream. Discover."

– Mark Twain

More from the Author

Two Sentence Business Plan — The powerful combination of a business plan, an action plan, and a to-do list, this workbook is an easy to use tool for anyone who wants to write a business plan that will help them start and run a profitable business.

Here's what some of the readers had to say about this workbook and the Two Sentence approach of writing a business plan.

"I love your 2 sentence concept for writing a business plan - your framework forces one to get to the meat of the matter which makes the business plan lean and lovely."

> - Suzen Sam,
> Social Media Consultant at HiddenGround.net

"This is a great roadmap that can help people move from planning (overplanning, over-researching, over-thinking, over-perfecting, etc...) where many of us stay stuck and get to the actions that will actually help us build a profitable business."

> - Tai Goodwin,
> Editor-in-Chief and Employedpreneur Advocate
> at LaunchWhileWorking.com

"I've never thought about writing my own business plan, simply because I thought it is really complicated, but with Devesh's "2 Sentence Business Plan", it was easy for me to write my own business plan. Thanks Devesh for developing this tool for business owners."

> - Sam Abdelmalek, Entrepreneur

This was the first time I ever actually felt excitement in the face of a business plan as opposed to the more usual dread.

> - Nicholas Lutsch, Entrepreneur

Get Your Copy at www.TwoSentenceBusinessPlan.com

Made in the USA
Charleston, SC
31 May 2014